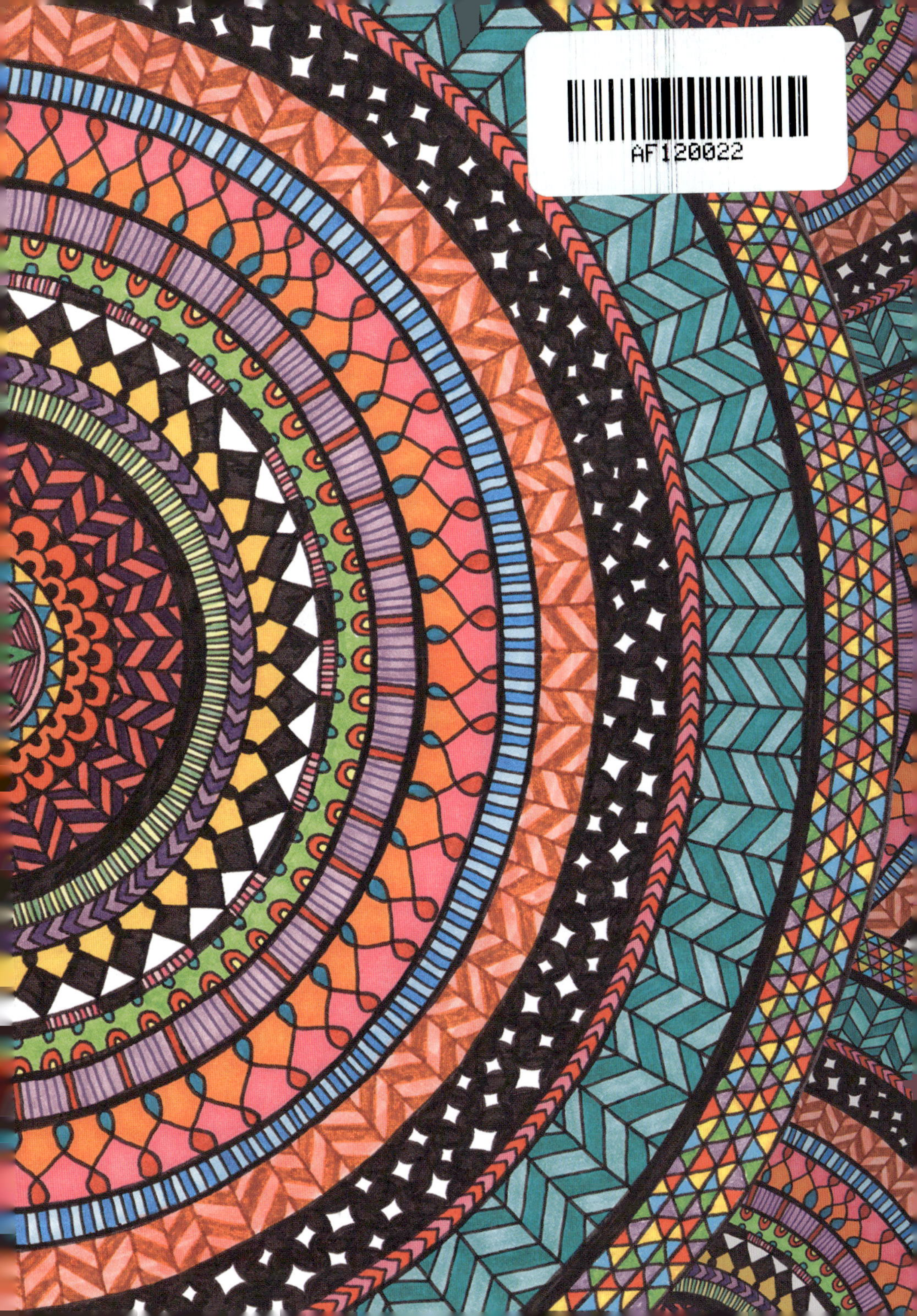

The wise thoughts of:

Writing in a journal is such a great way to capture special thoughts and memories. It also helps spark my creativity. Hoping you find as much joy in keeping a journal as I do.

— hello angel

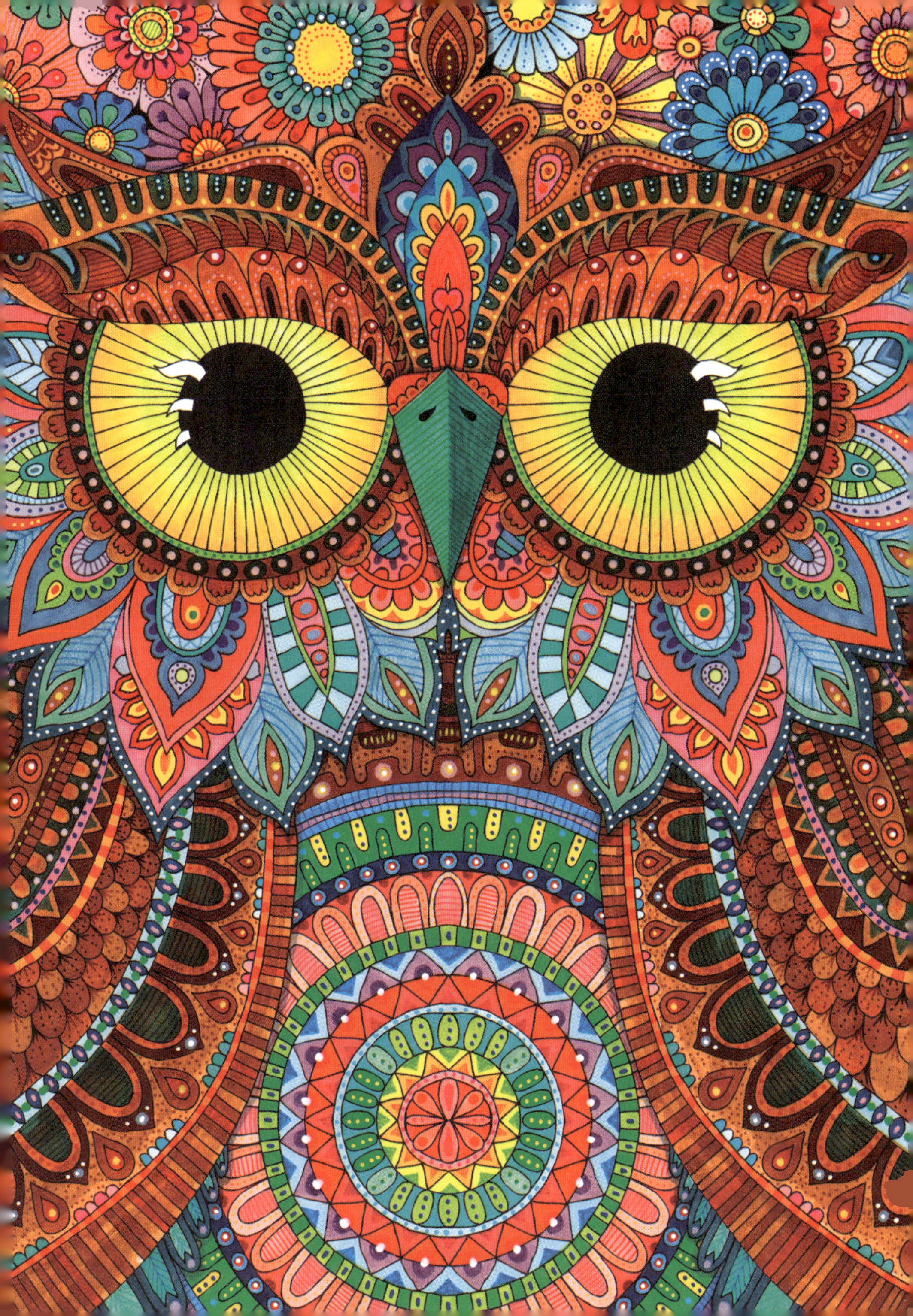

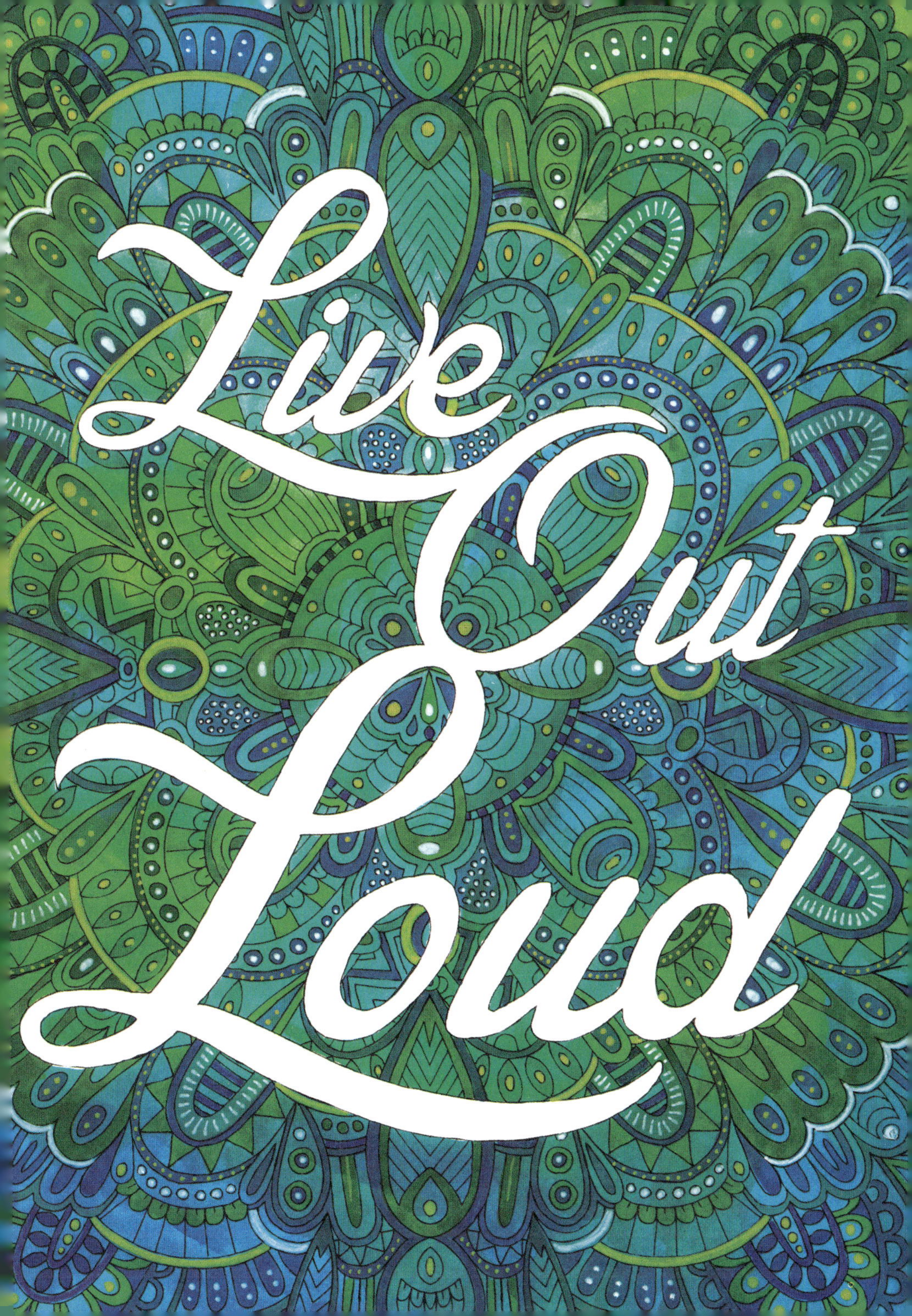
Live Out Loud

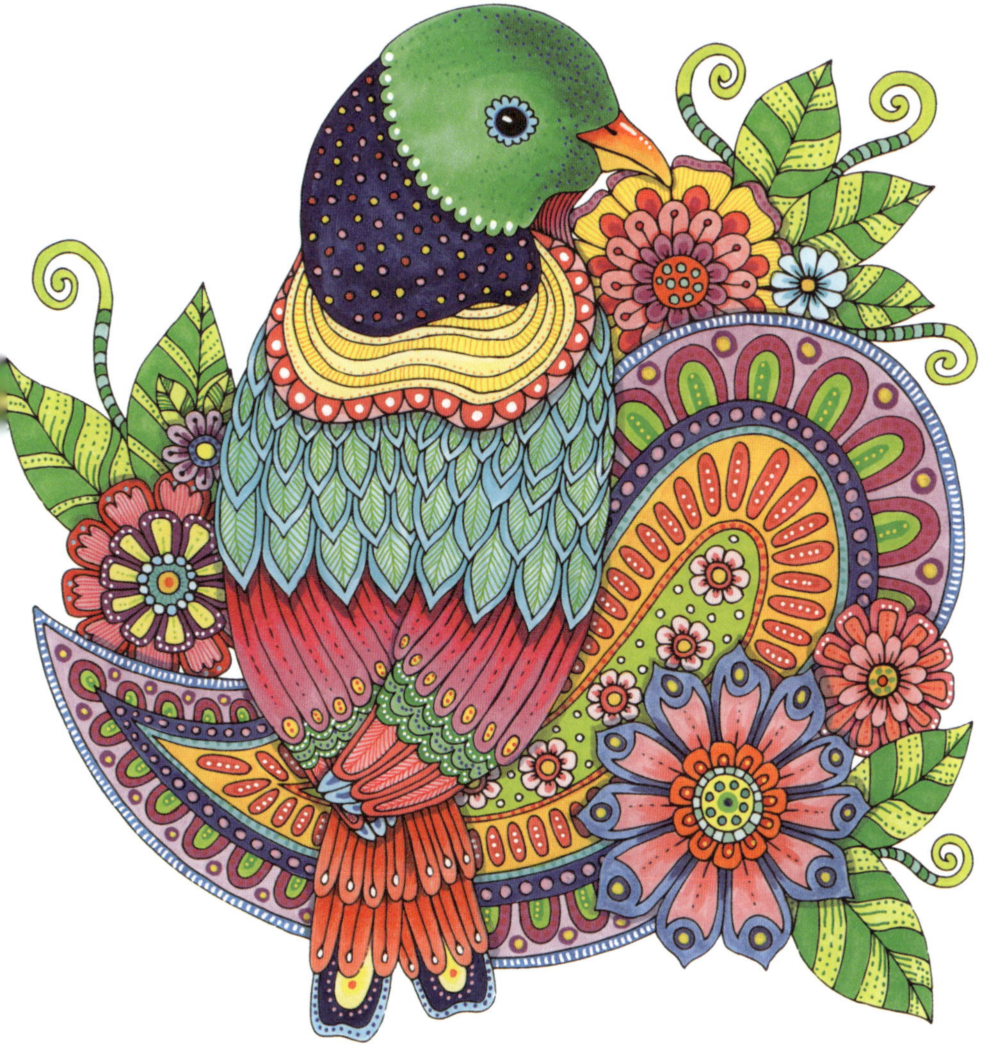

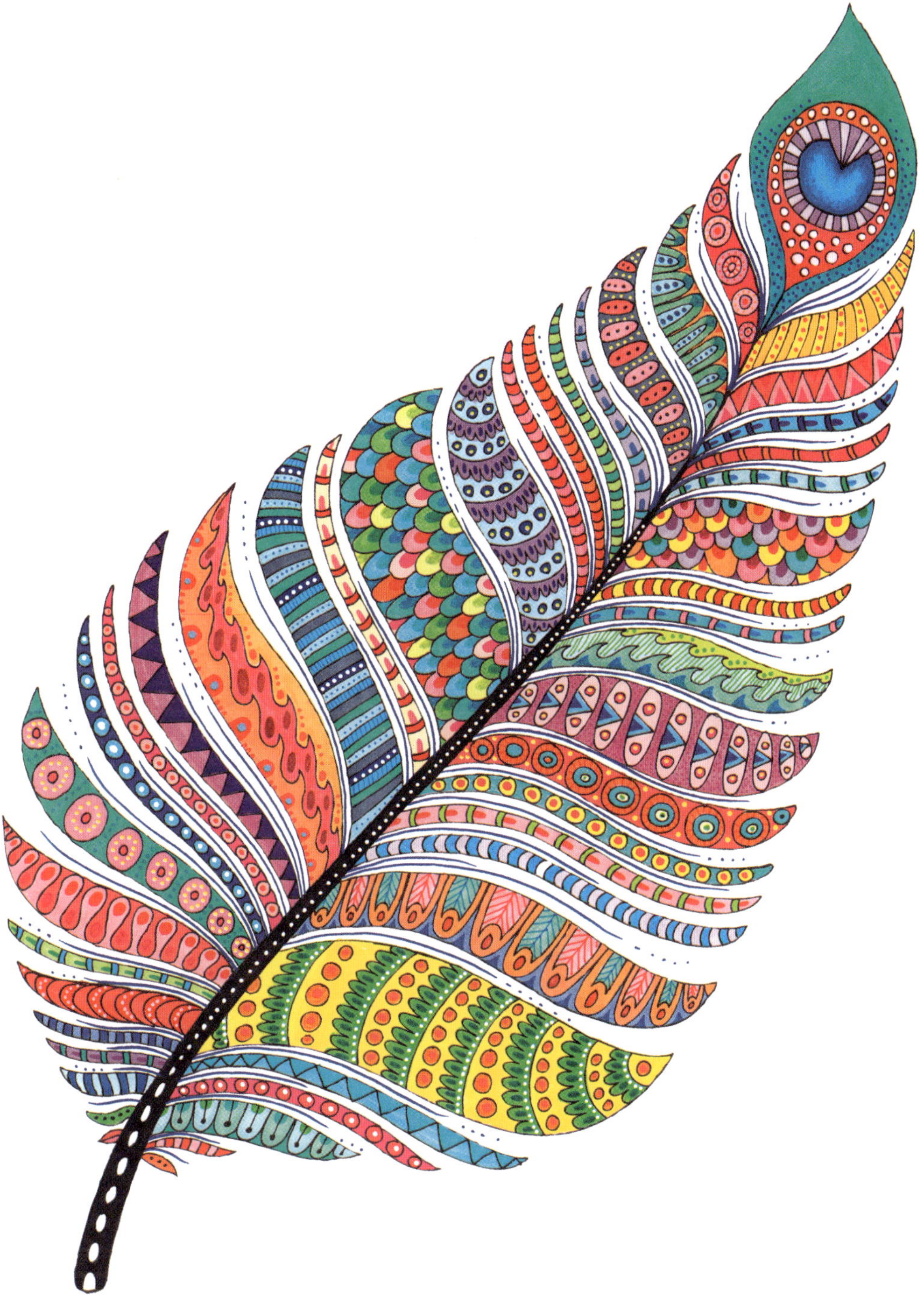

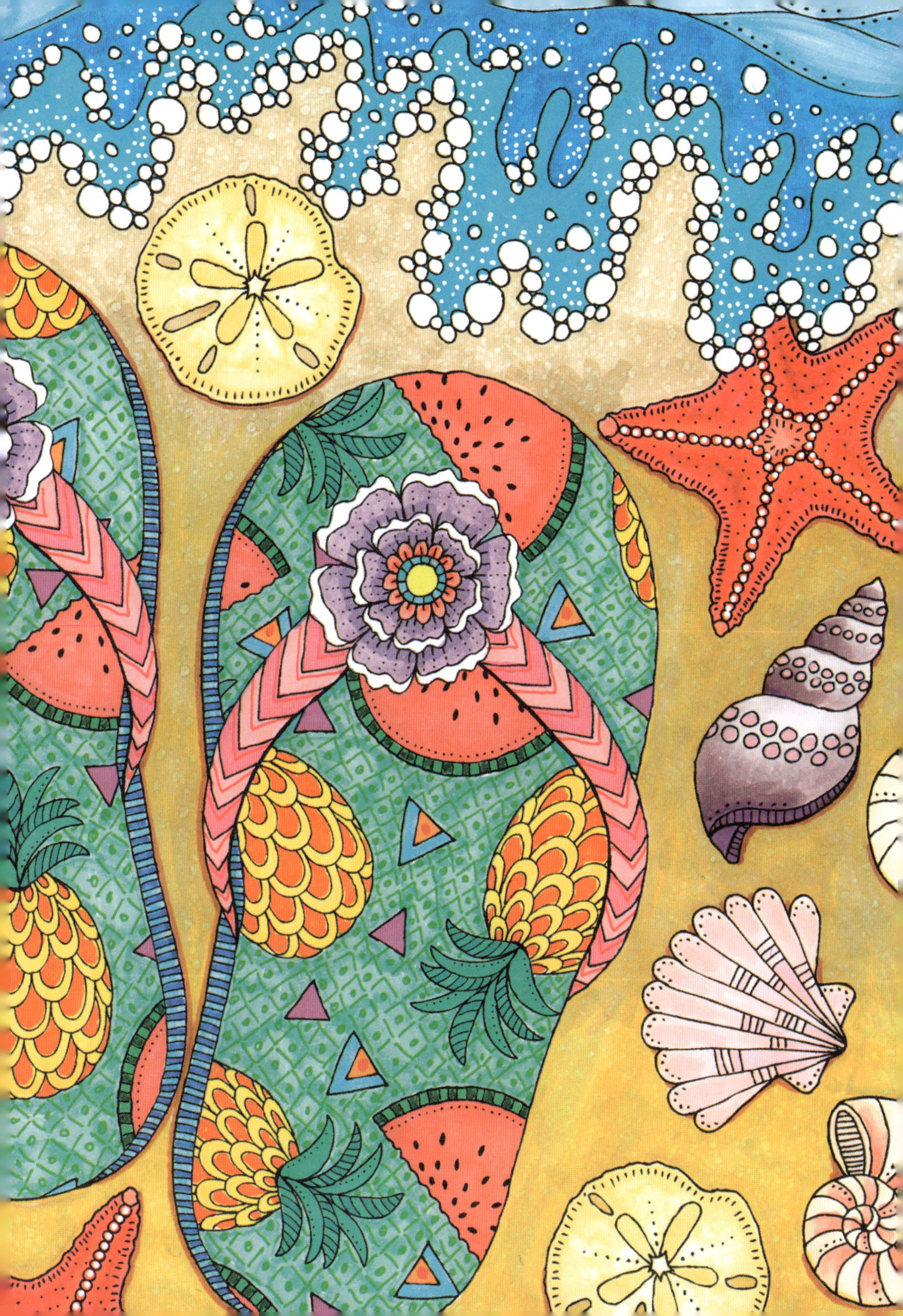

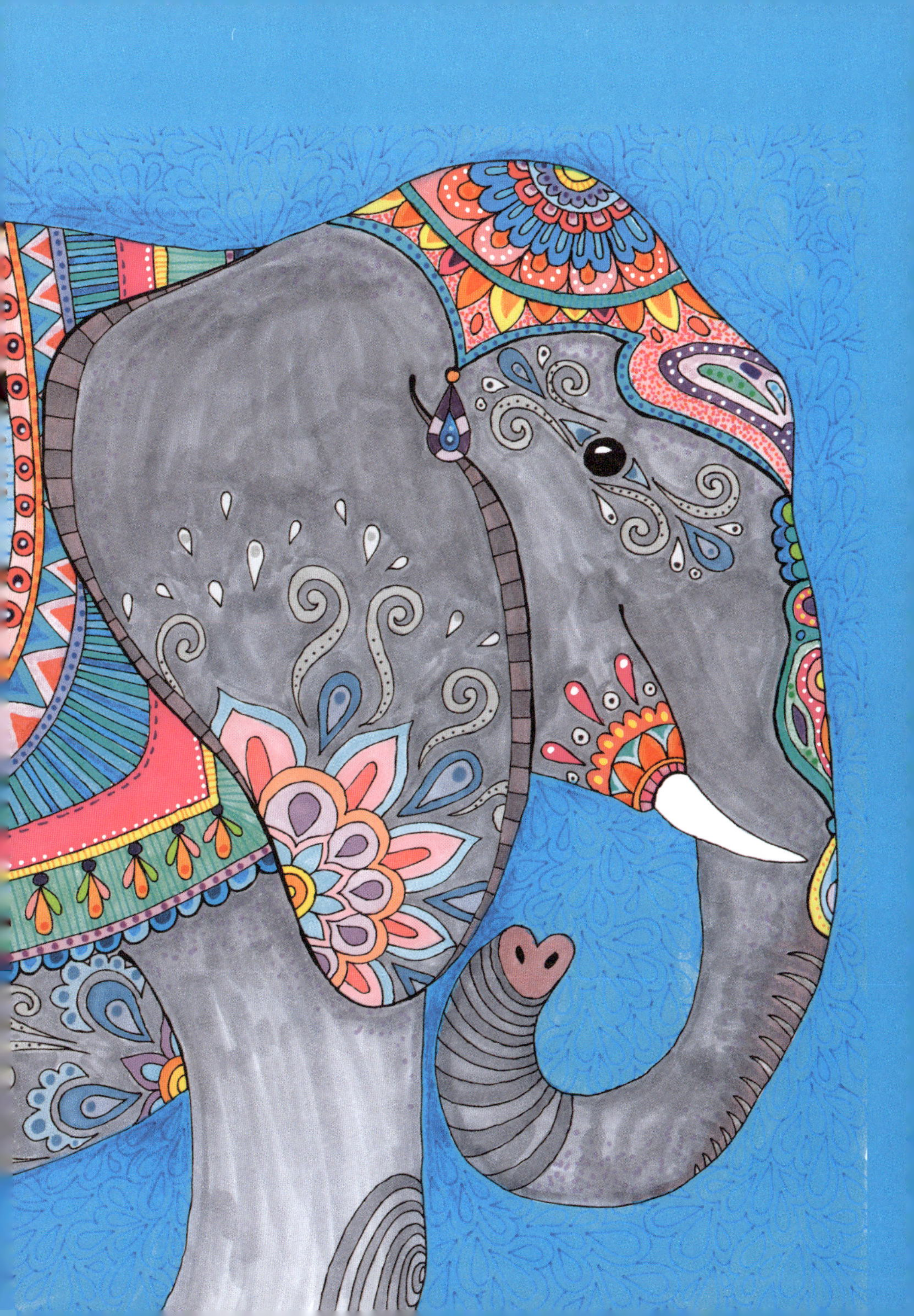

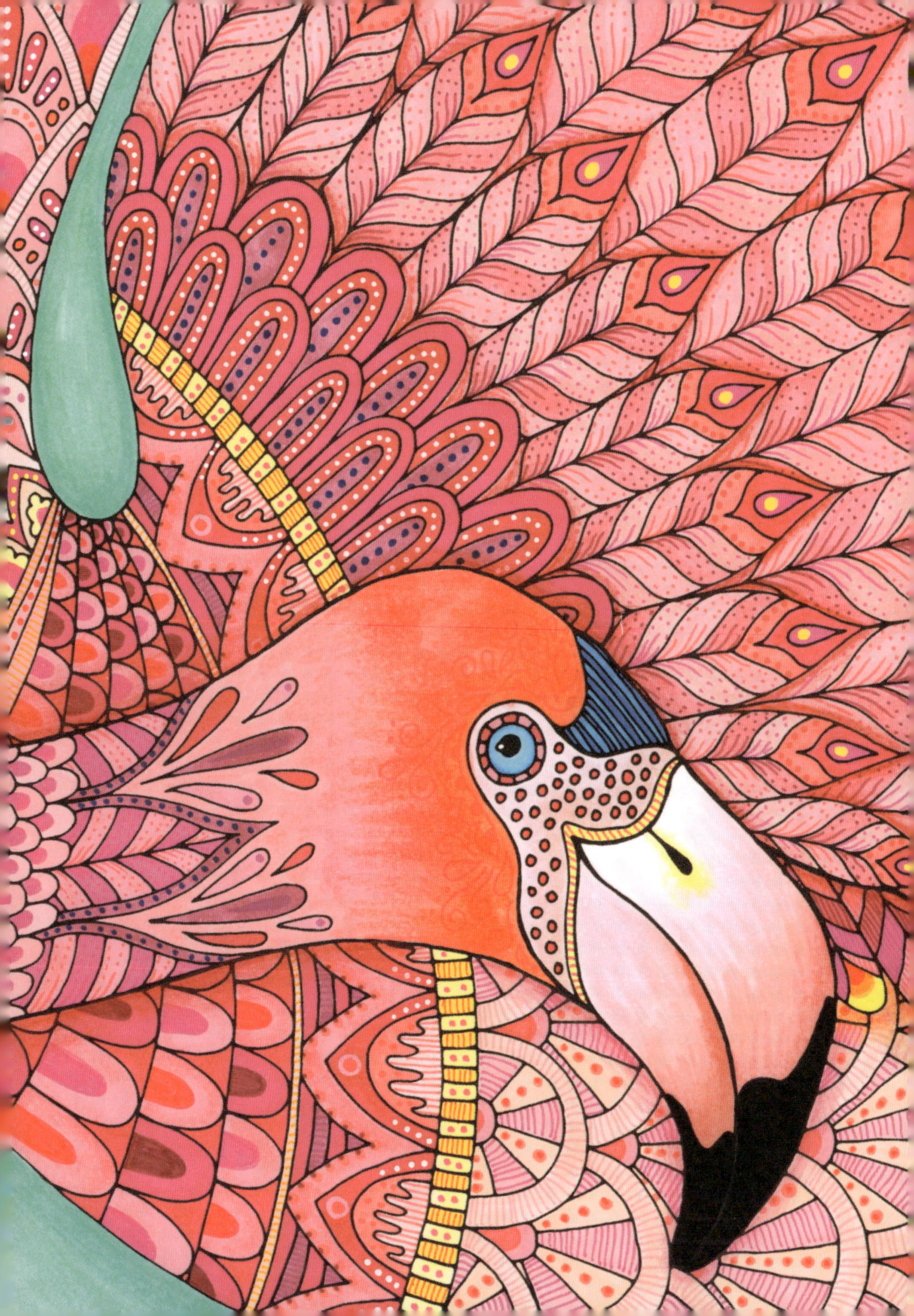

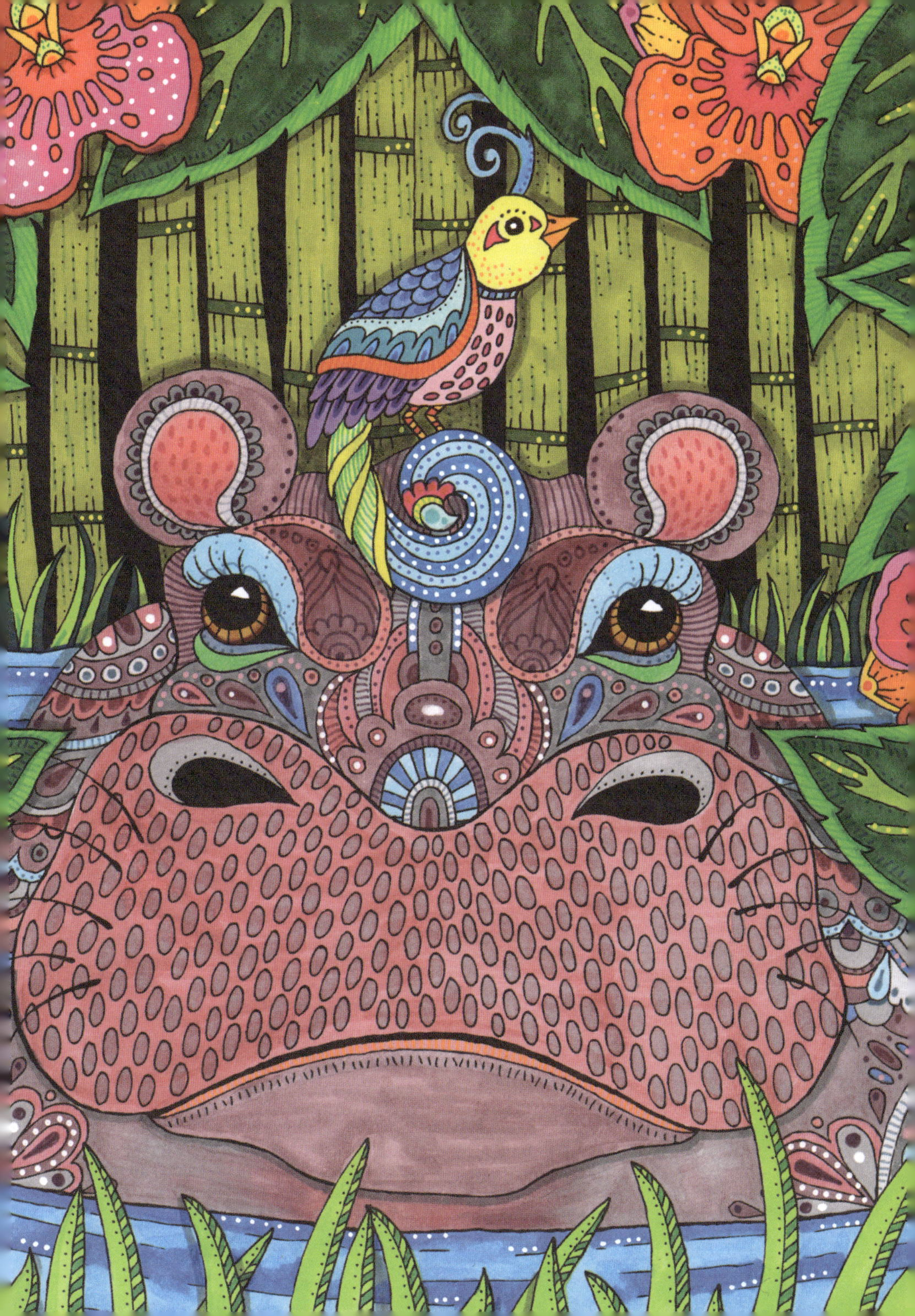

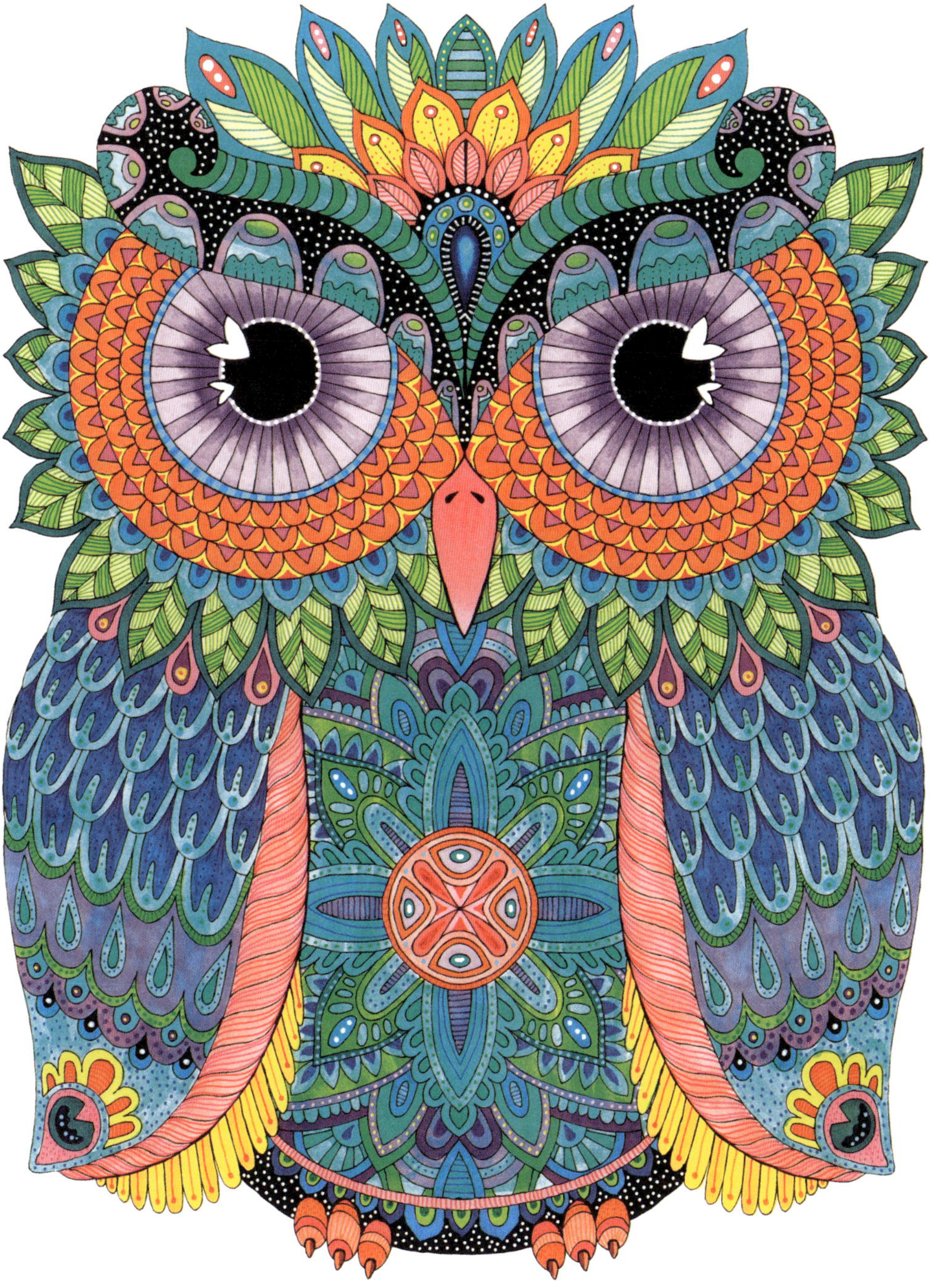

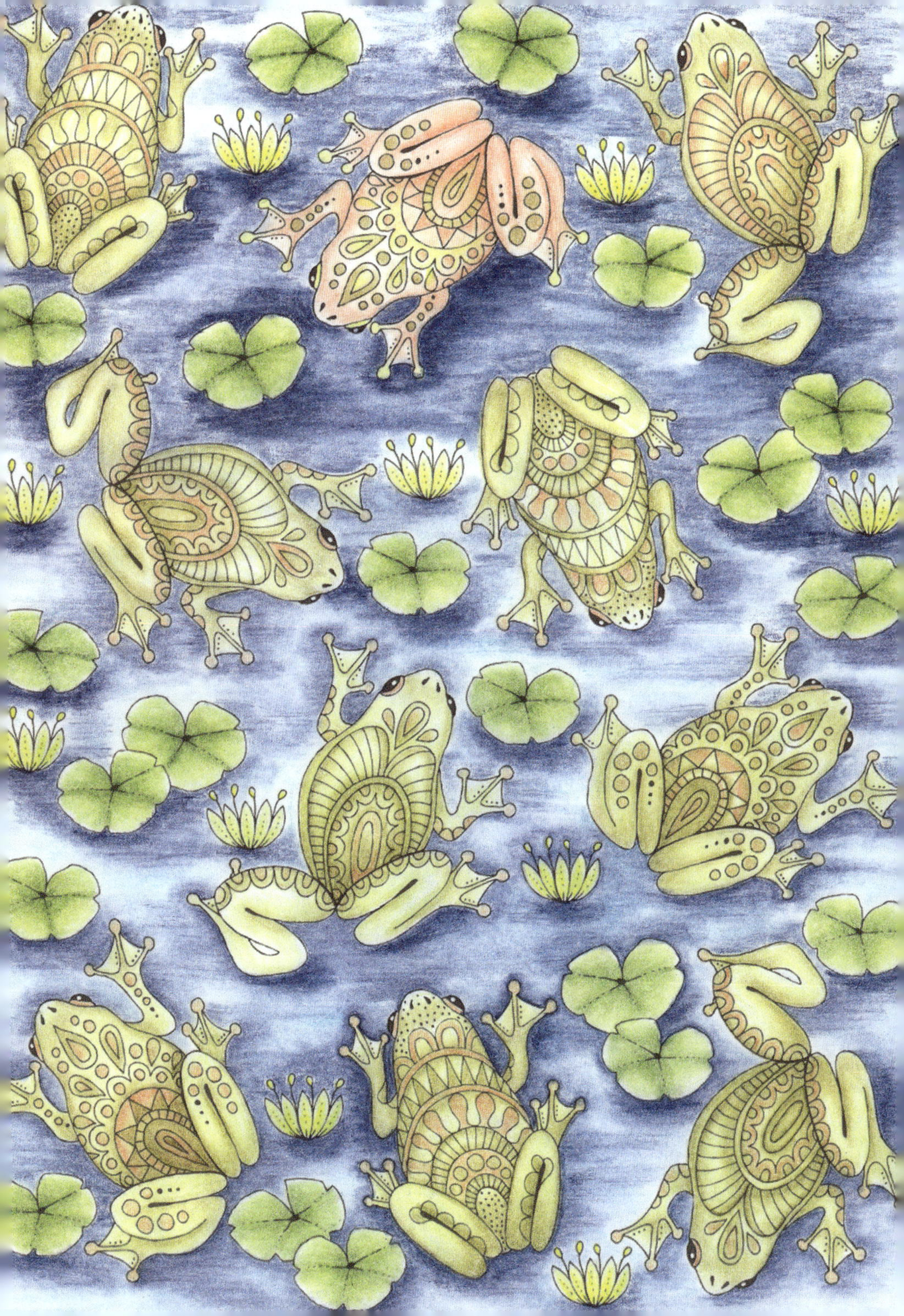

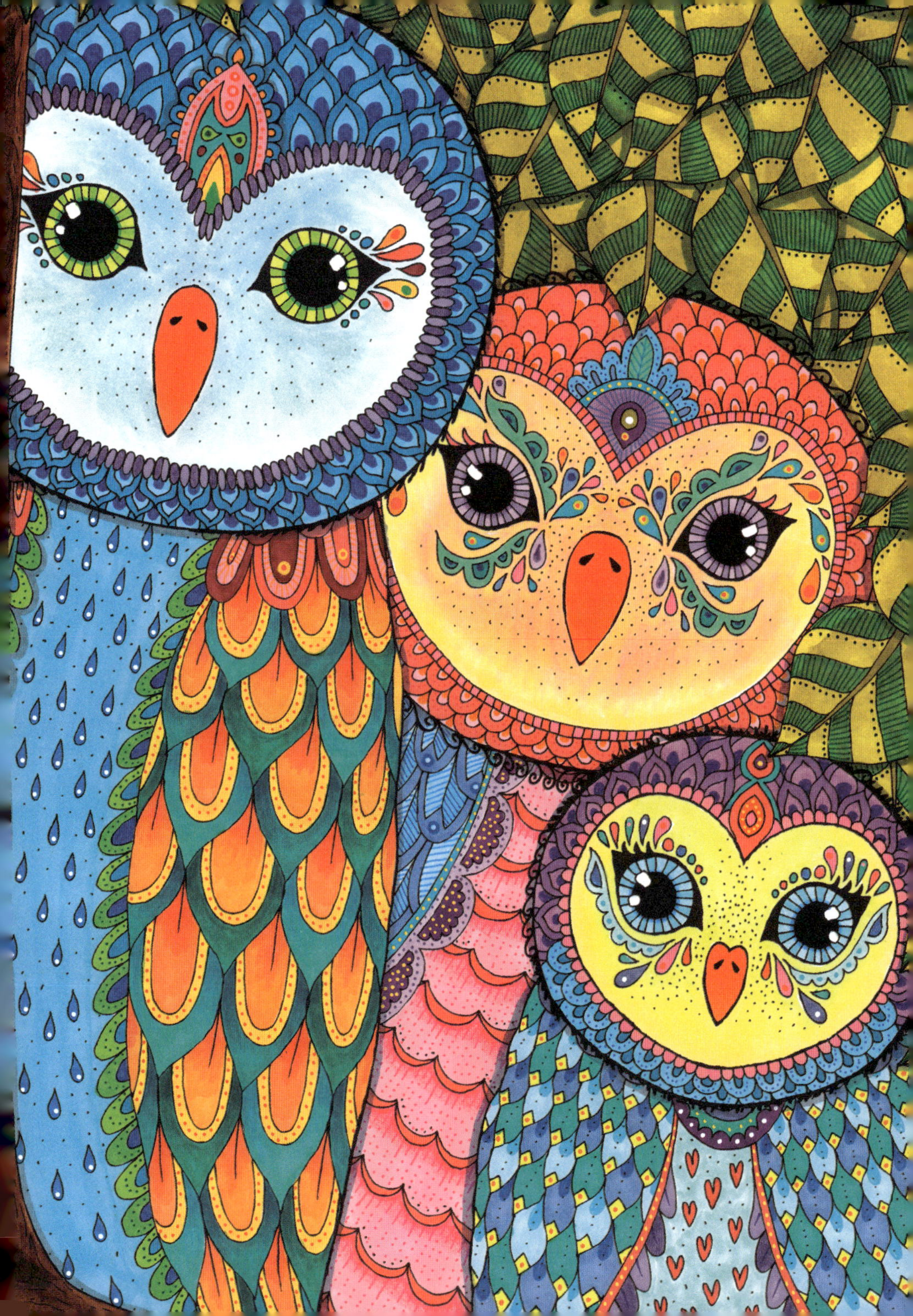

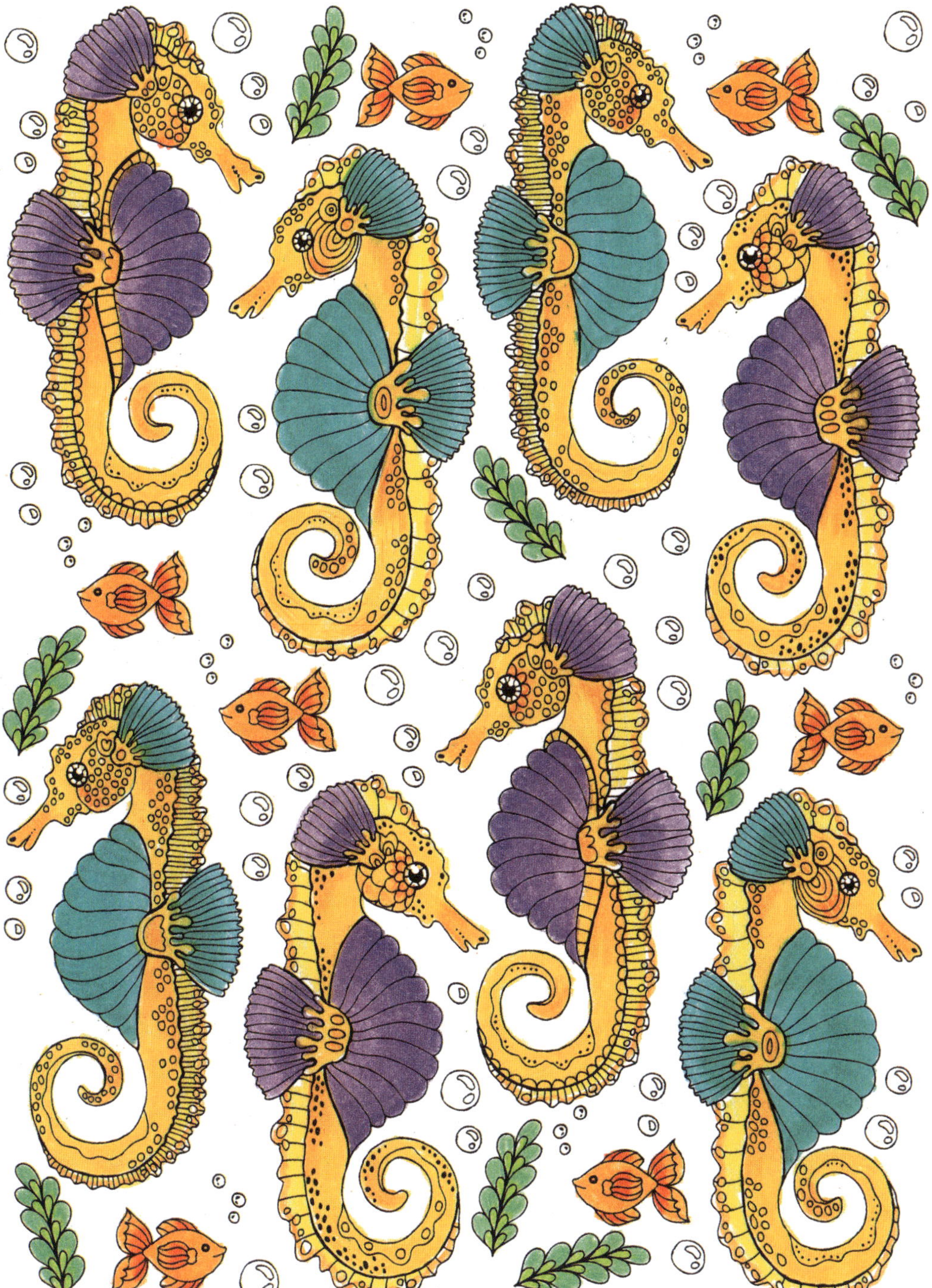

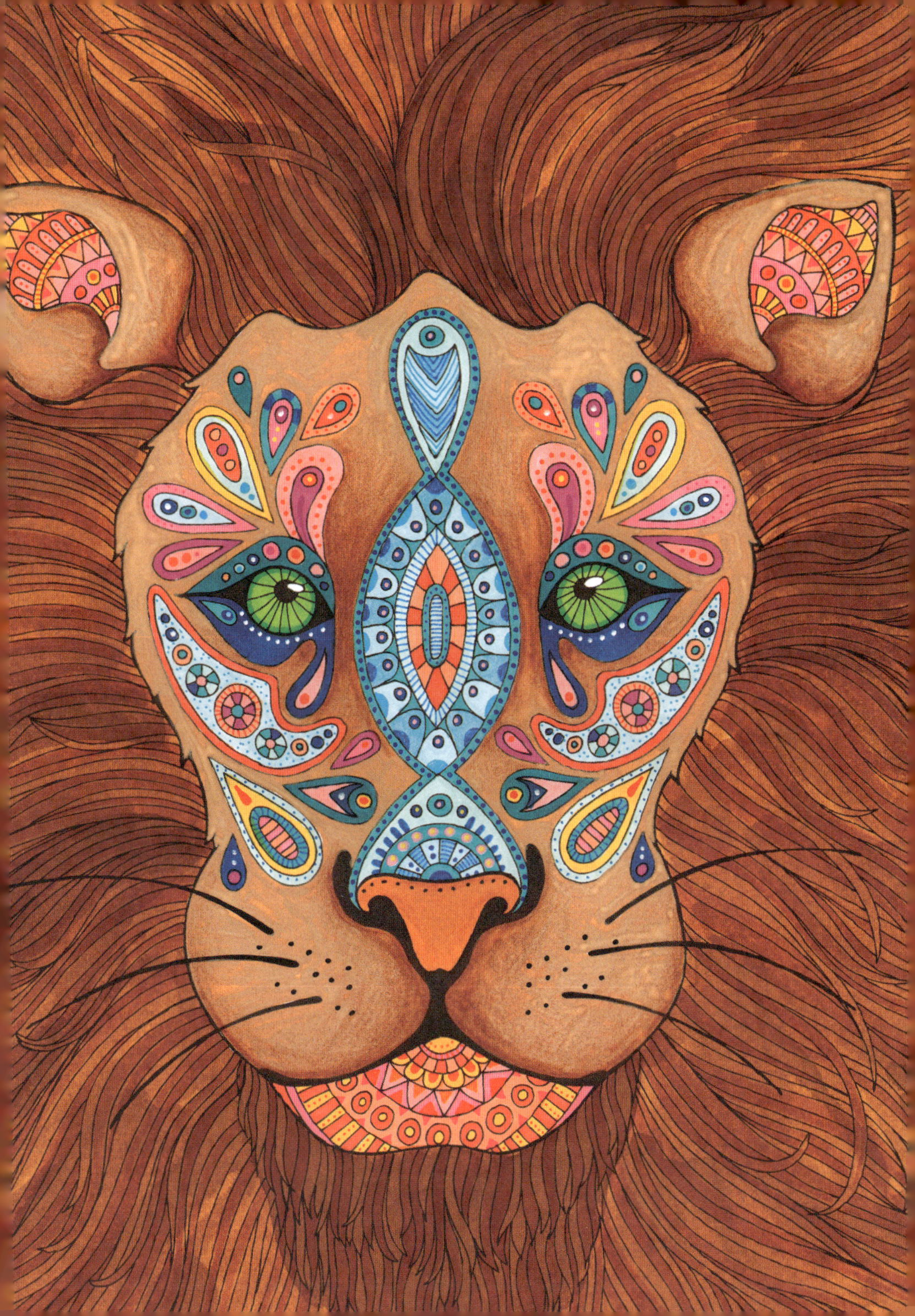

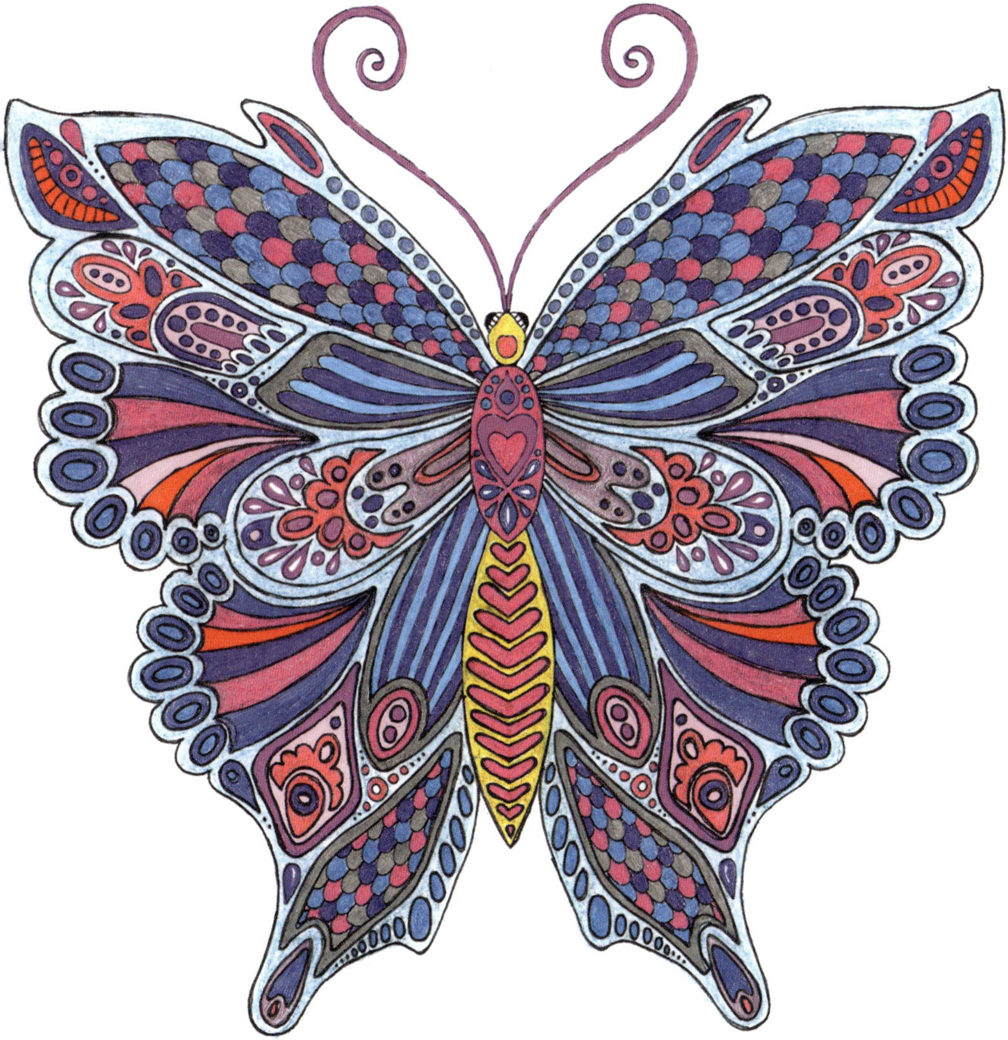

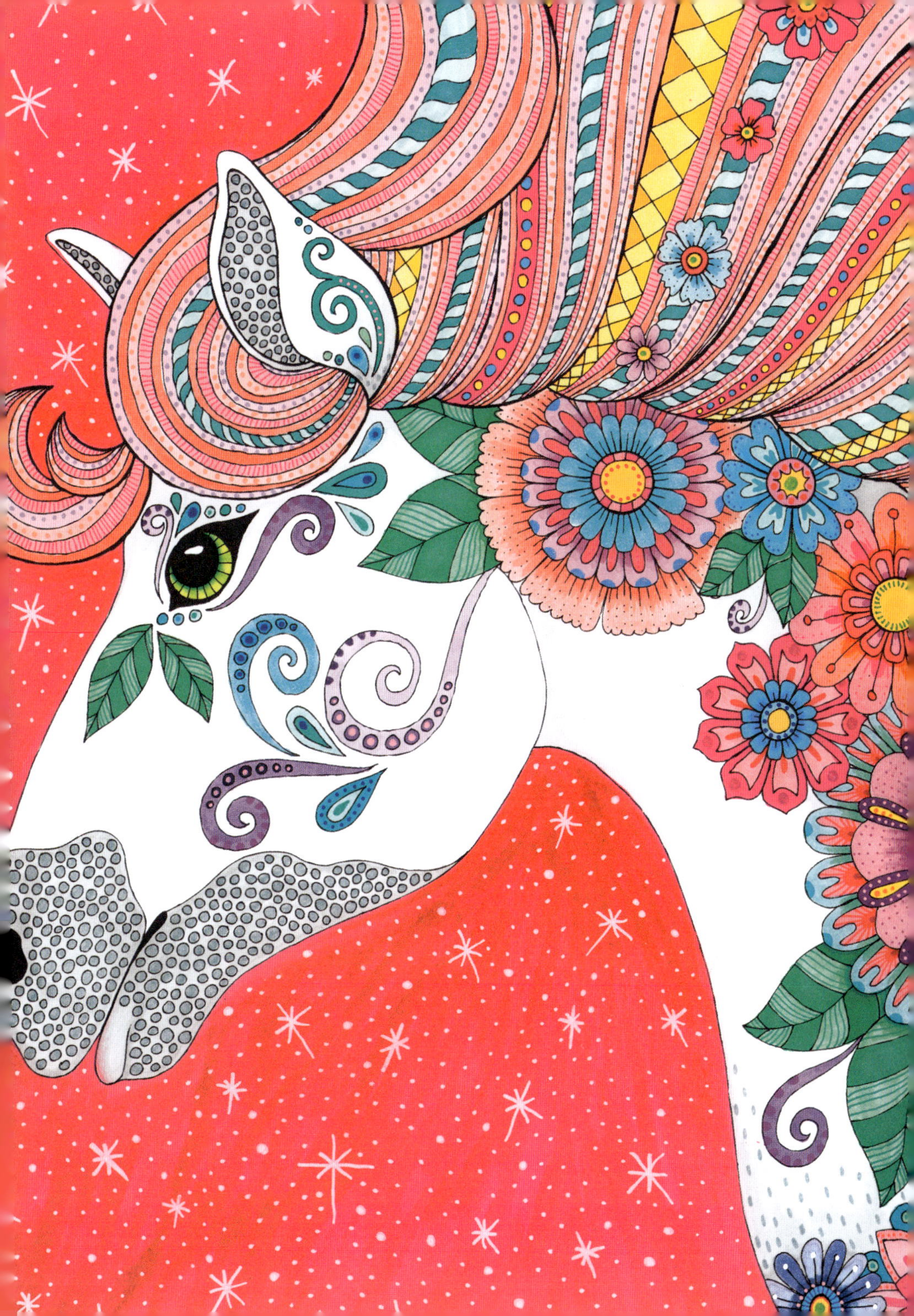

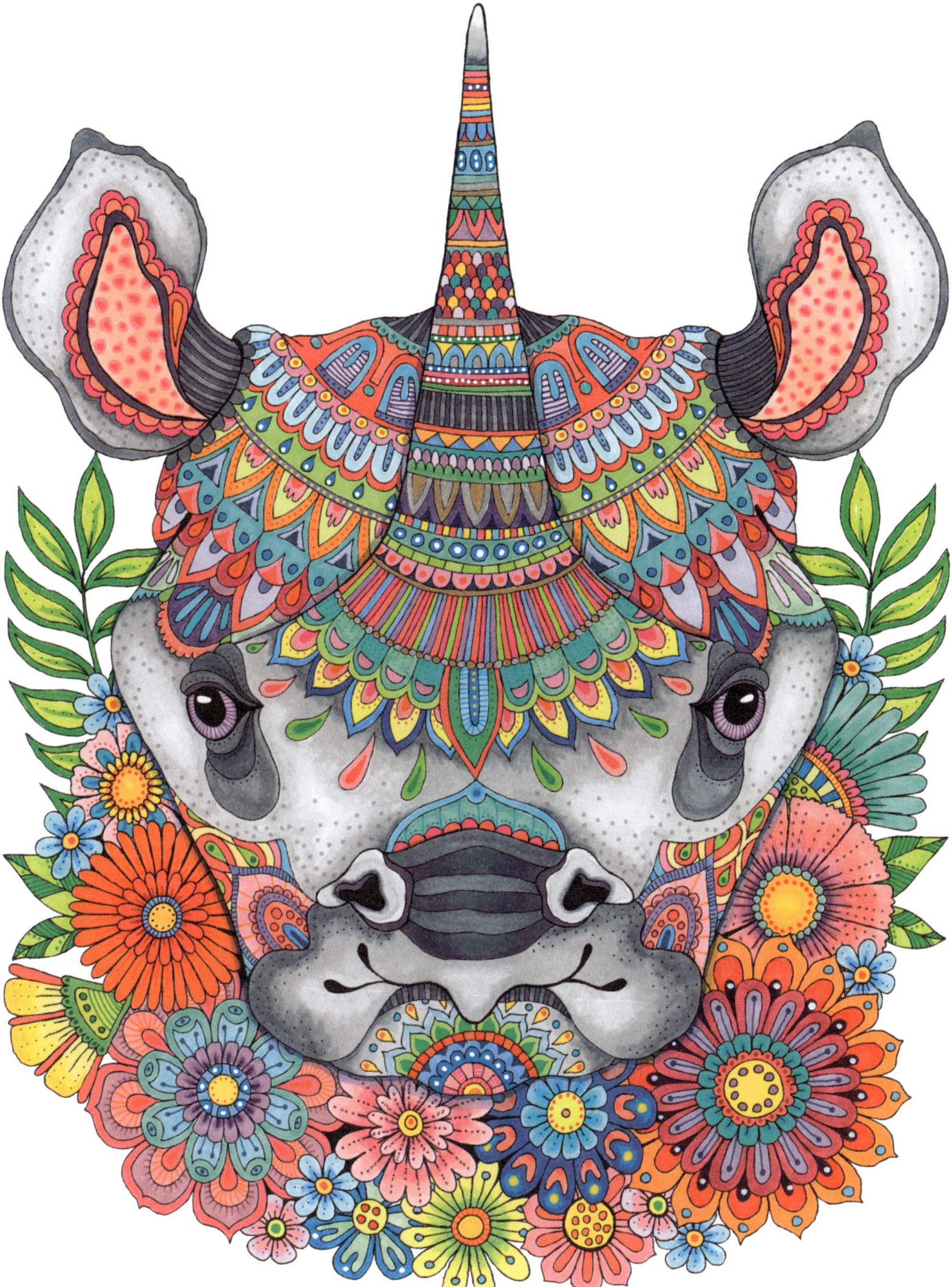

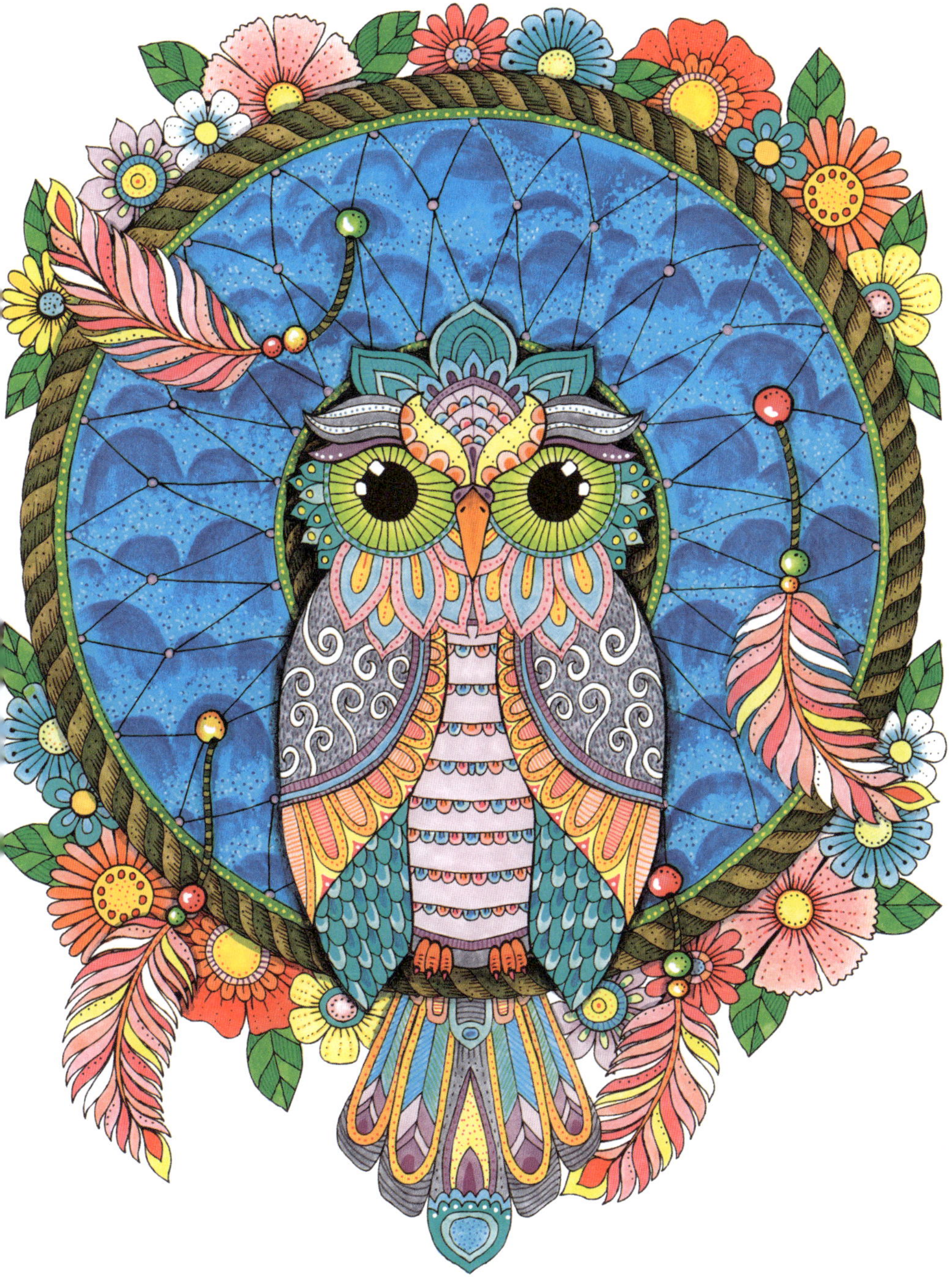

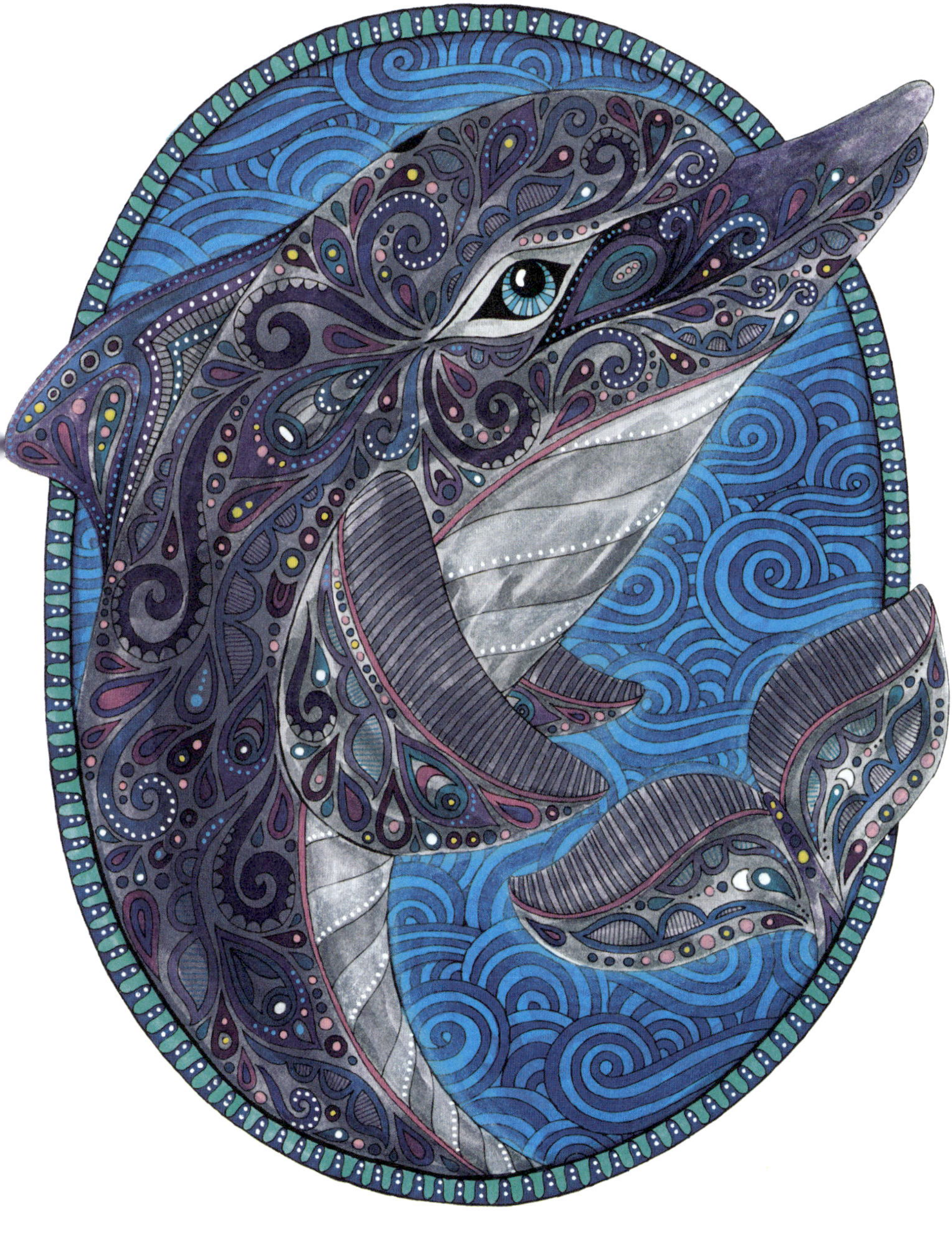

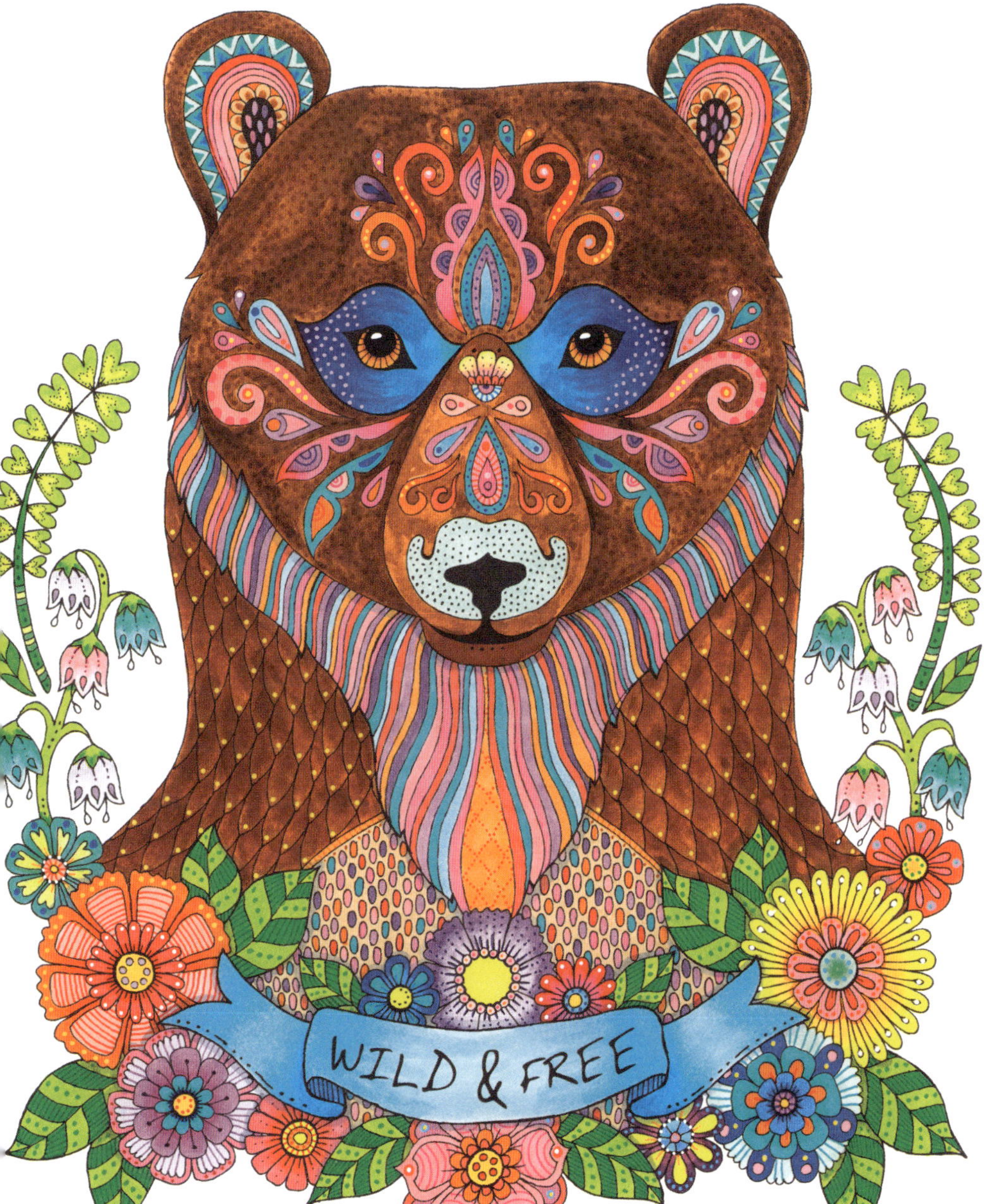
WILD & FREE

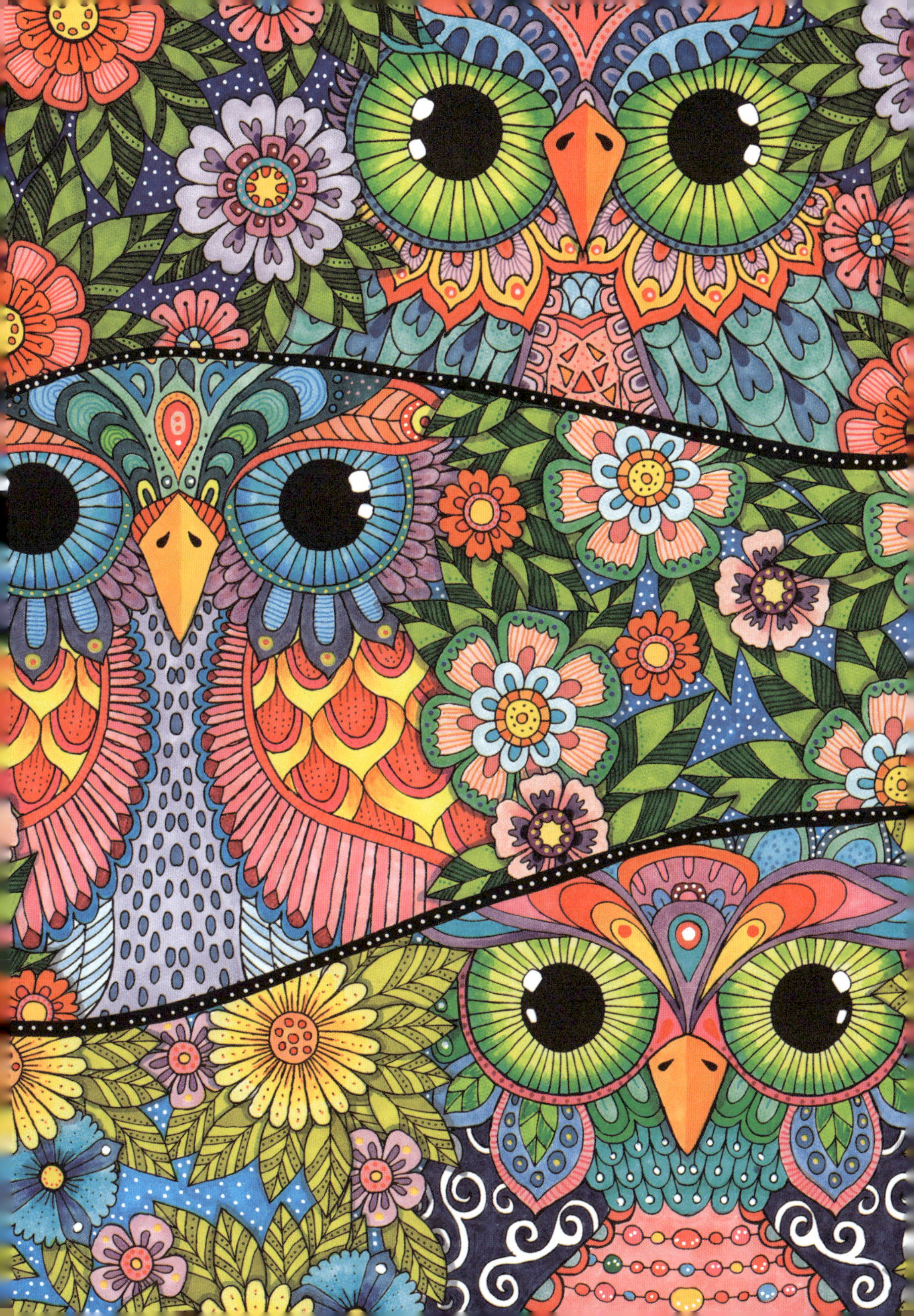

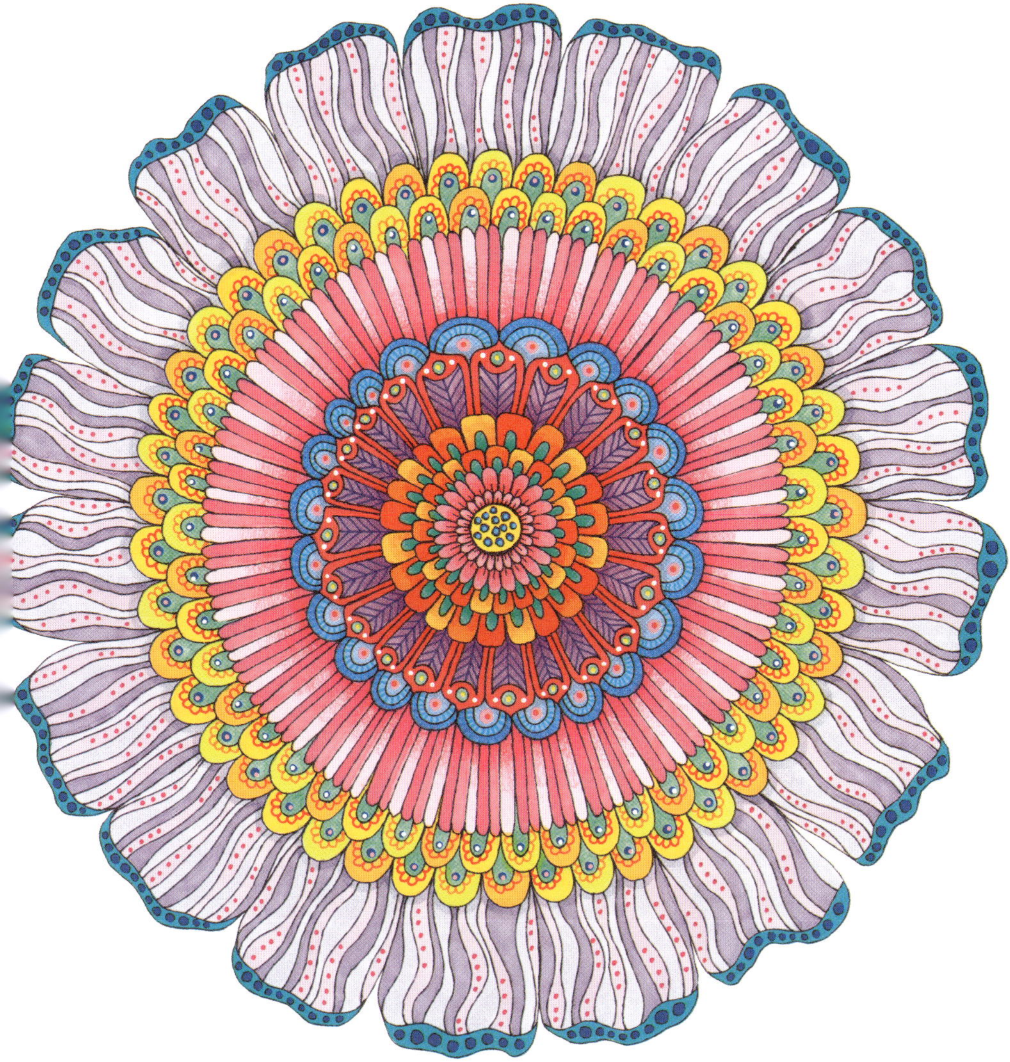

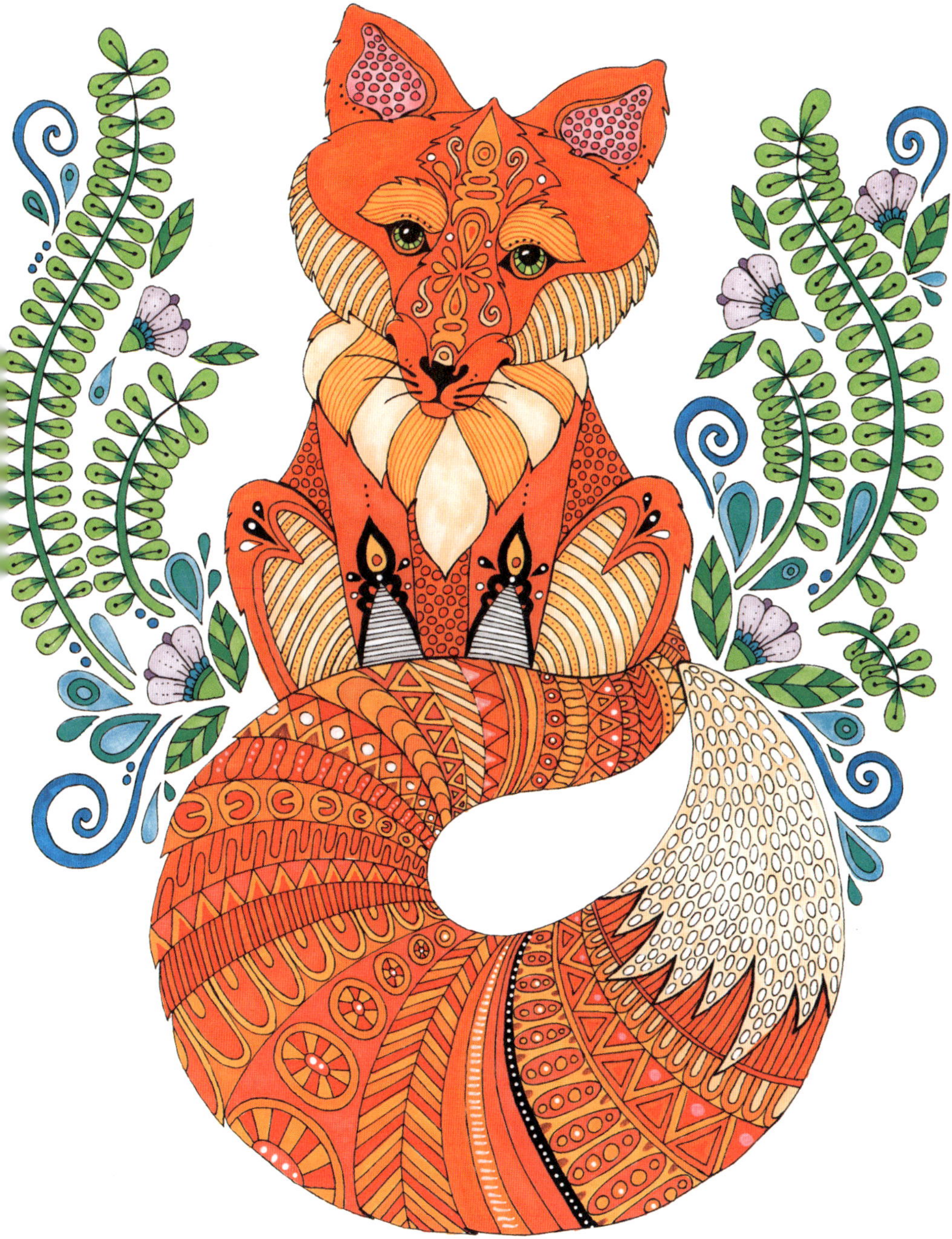

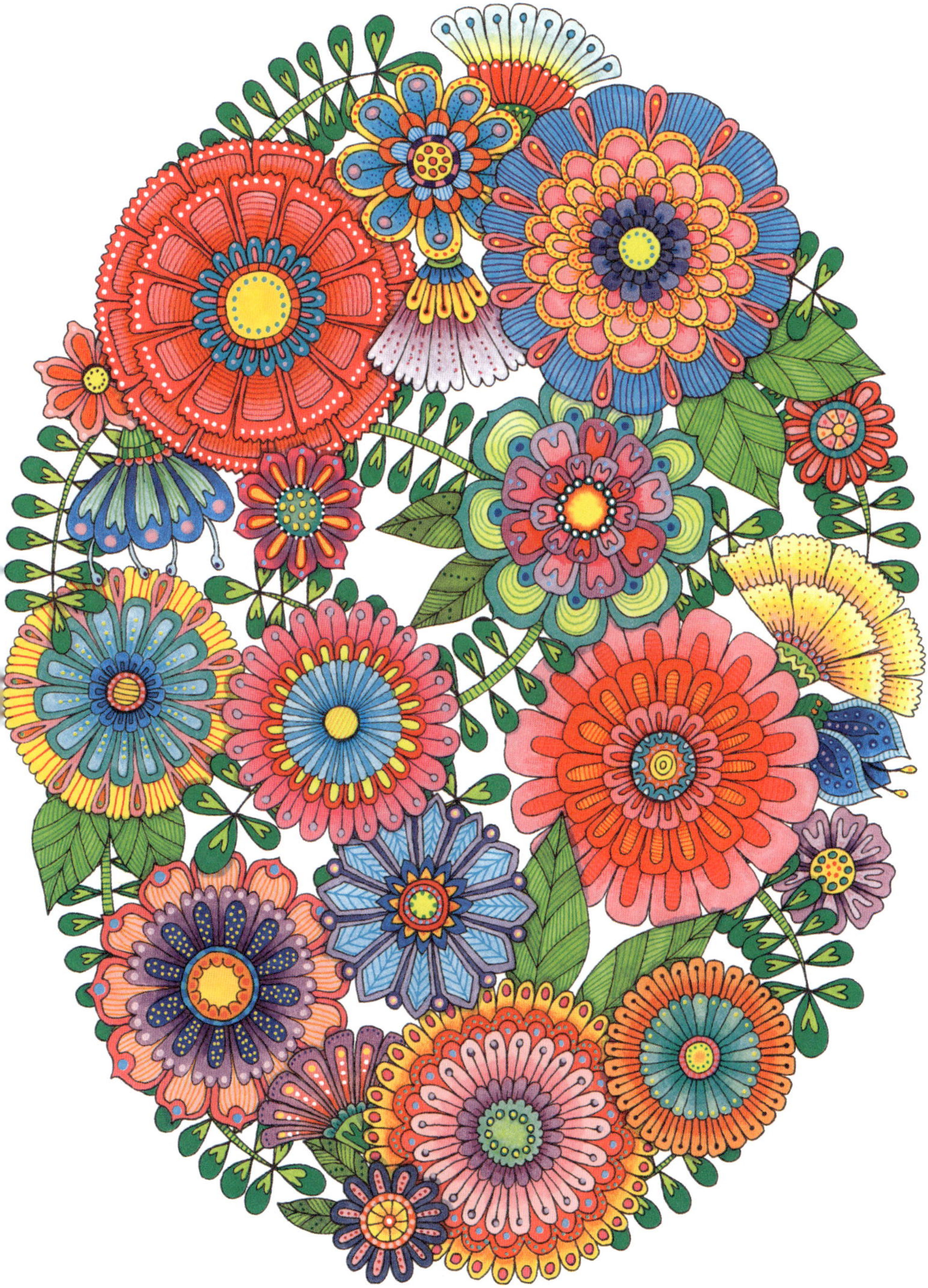

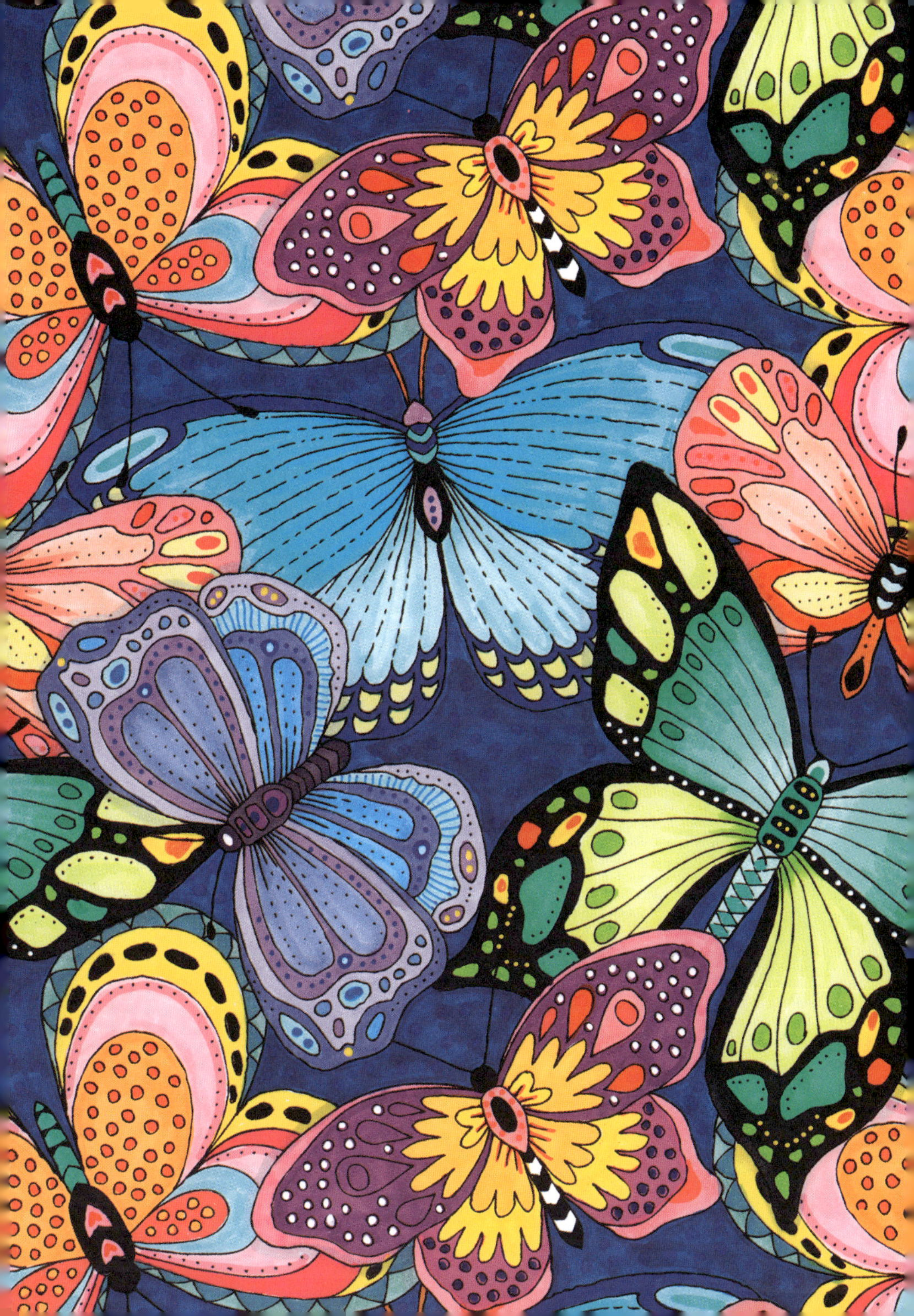

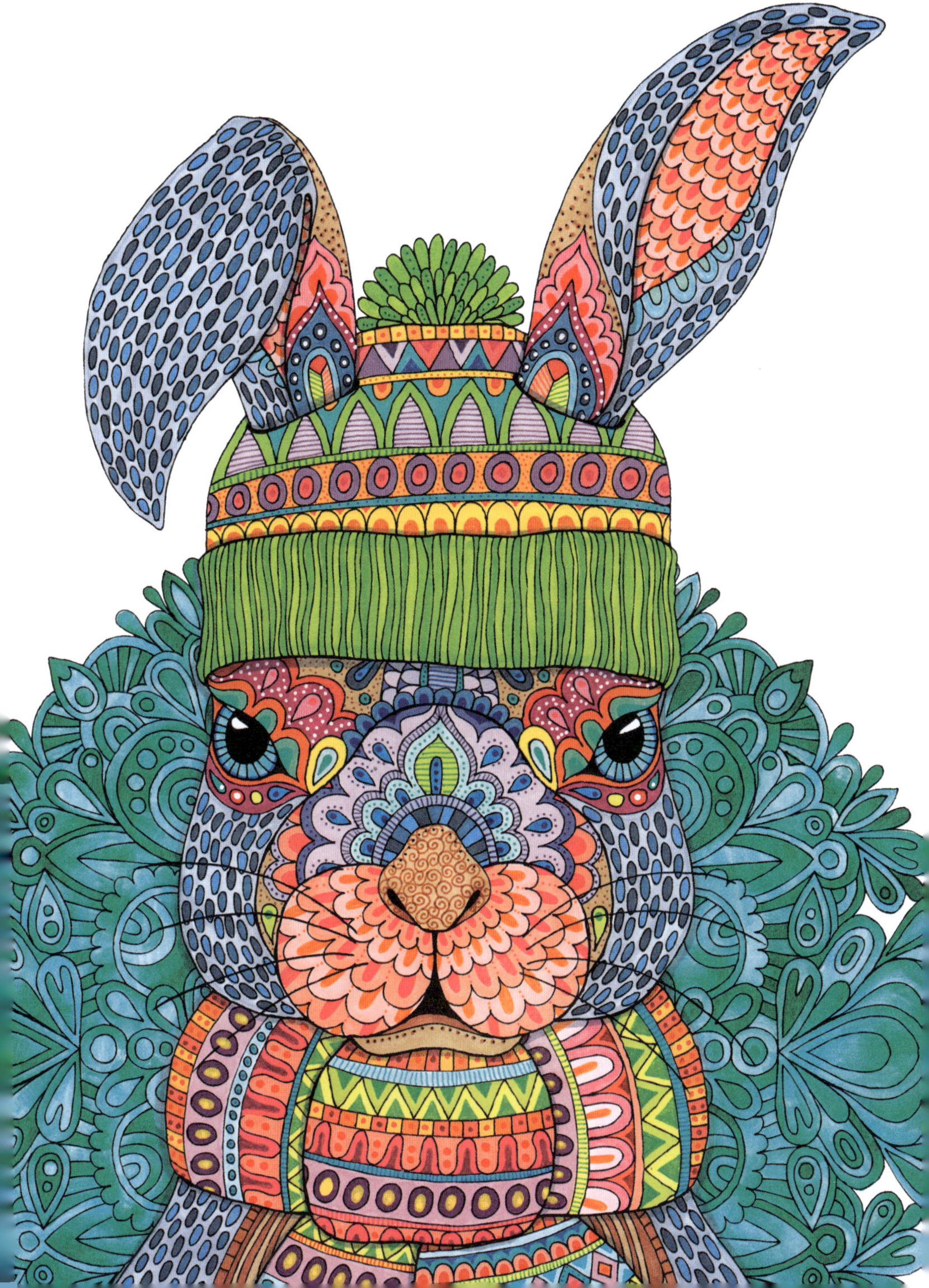

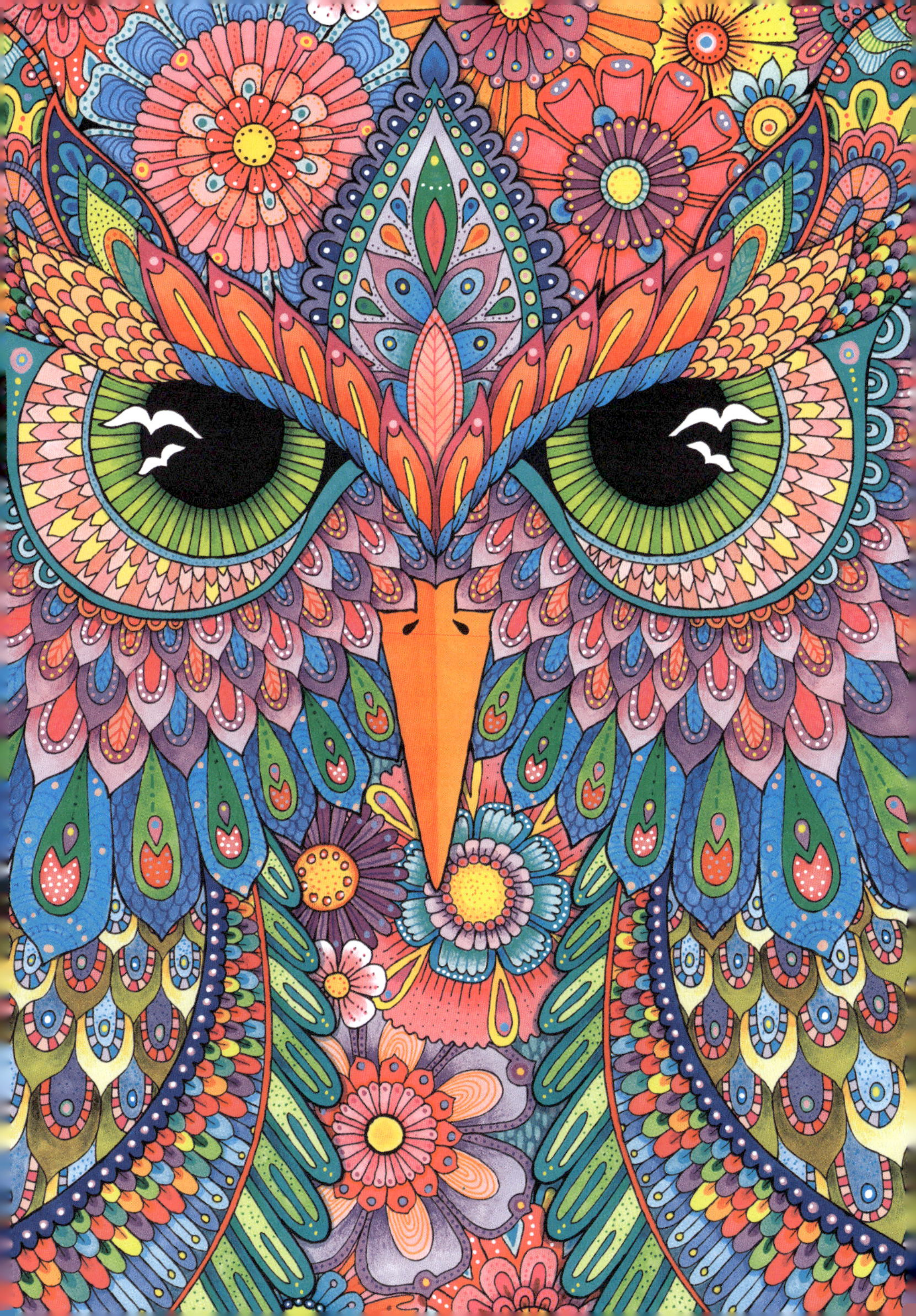

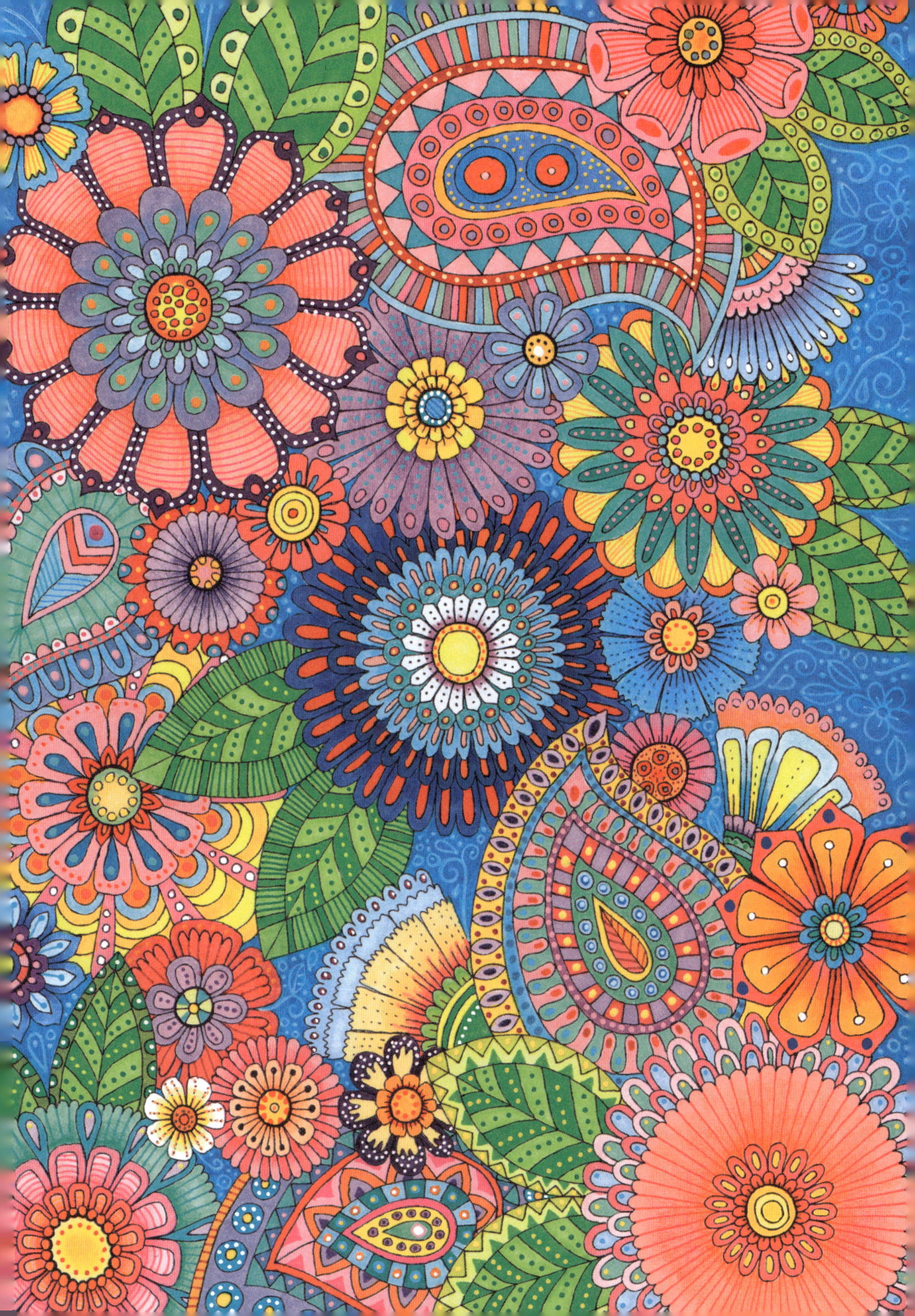

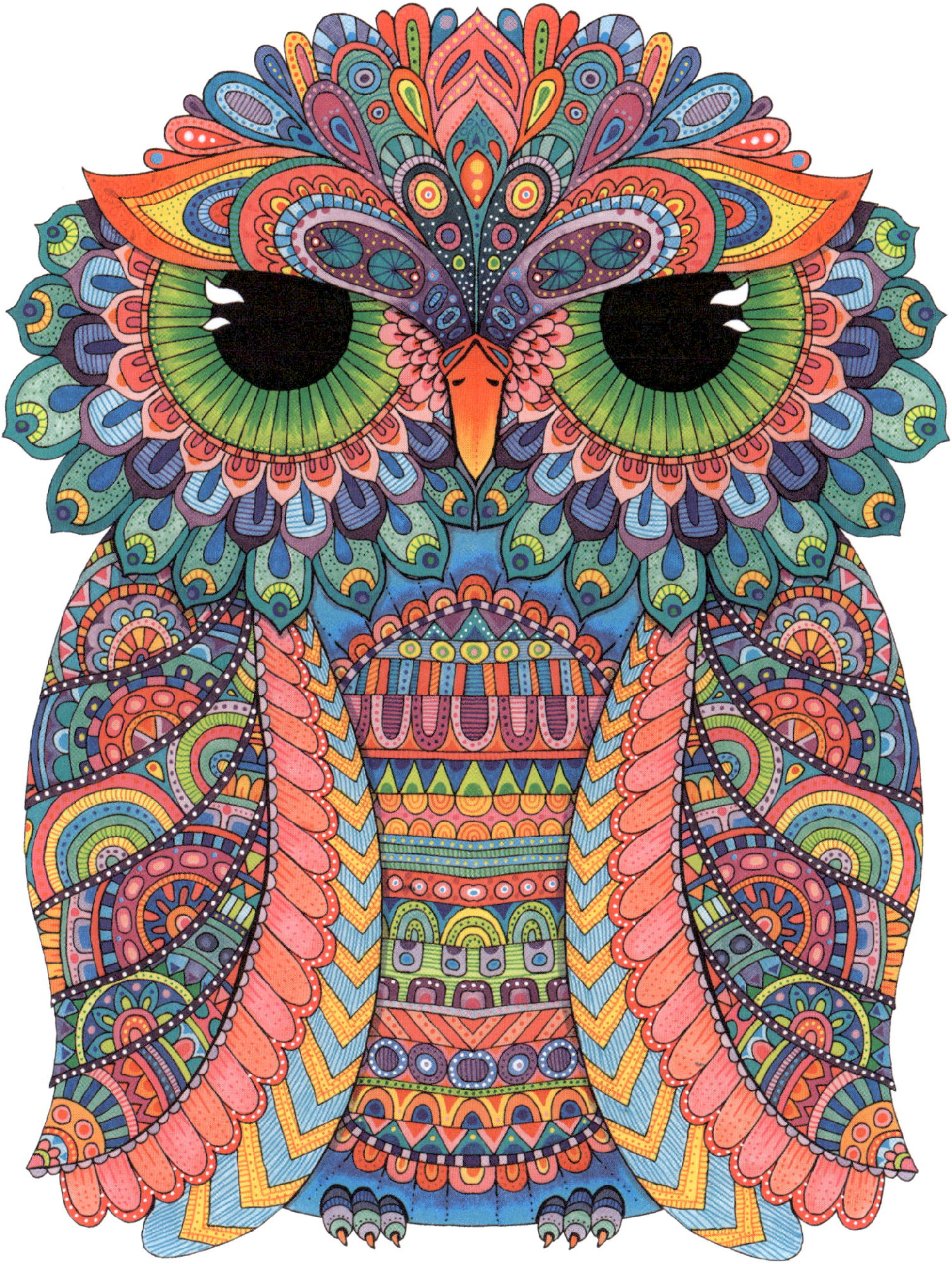

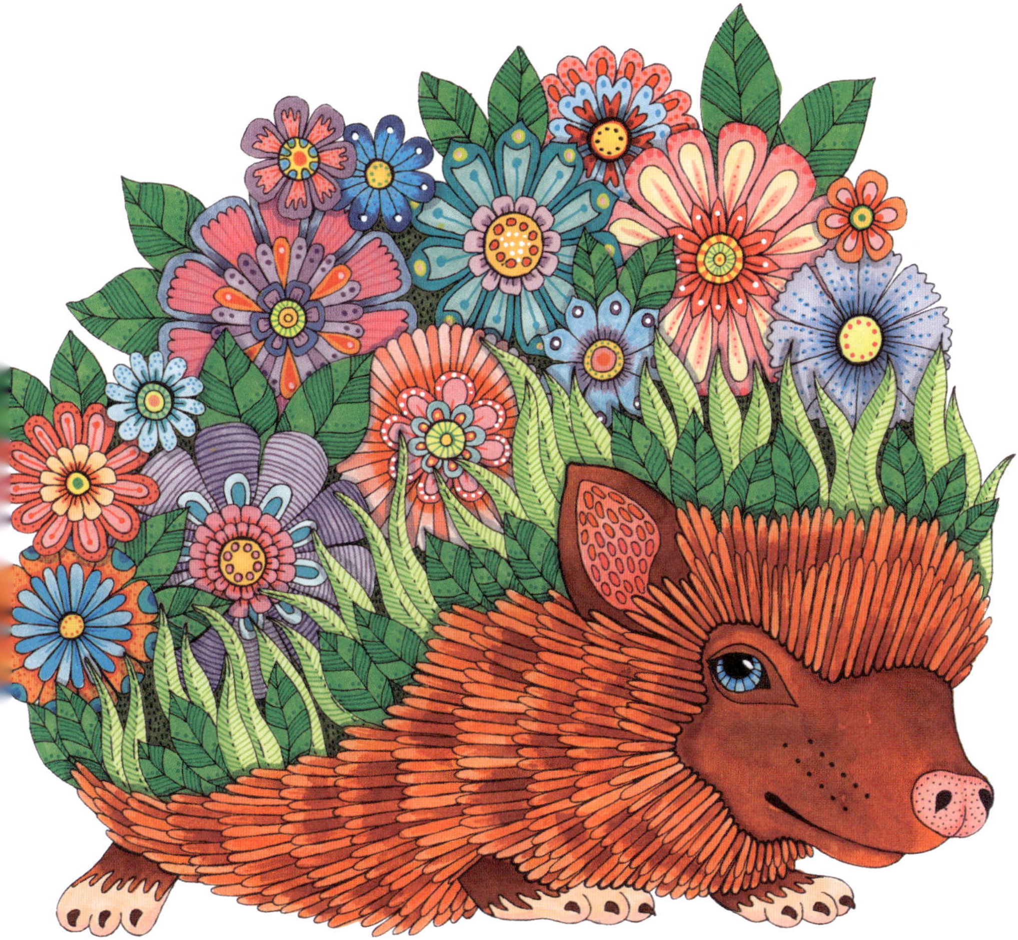

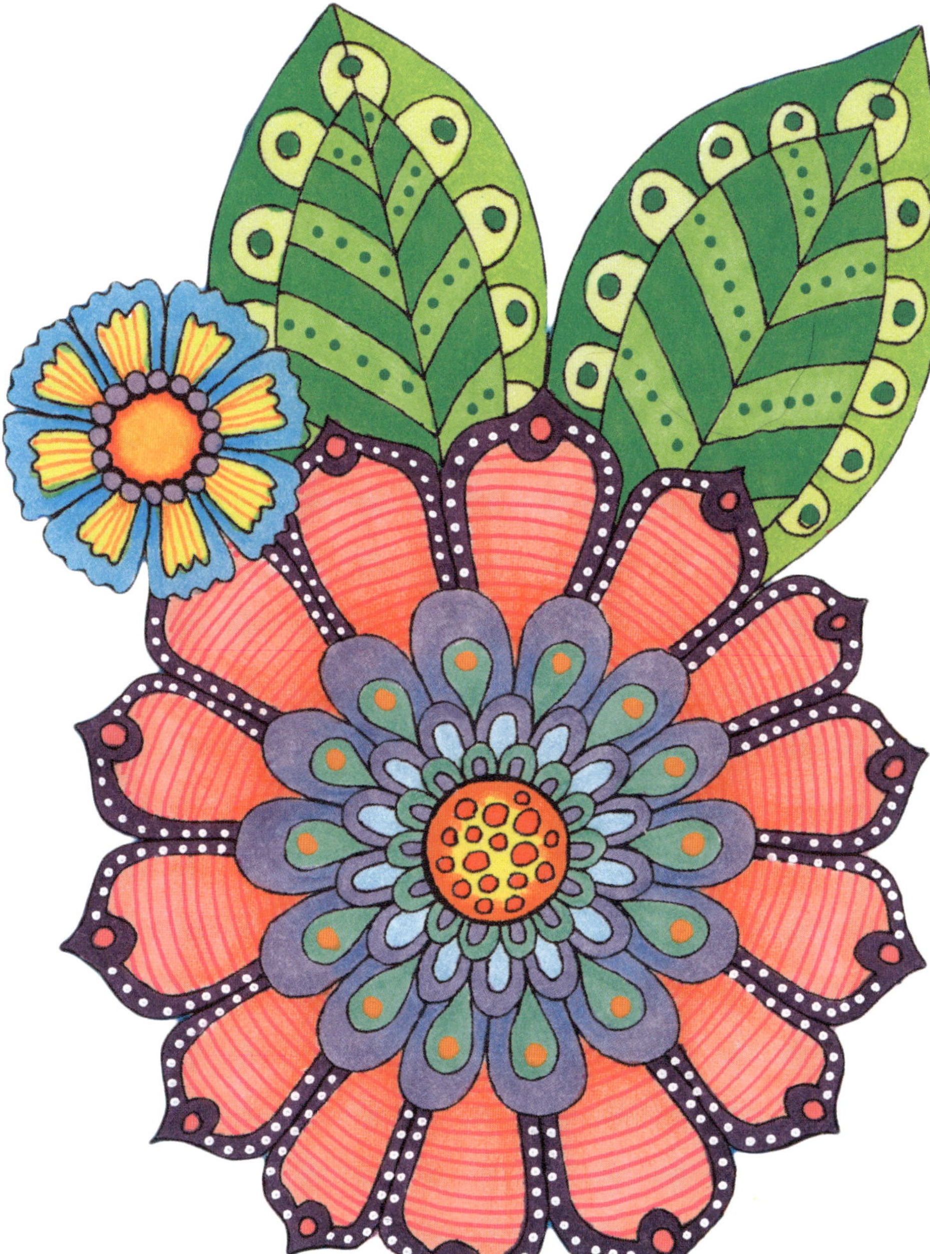

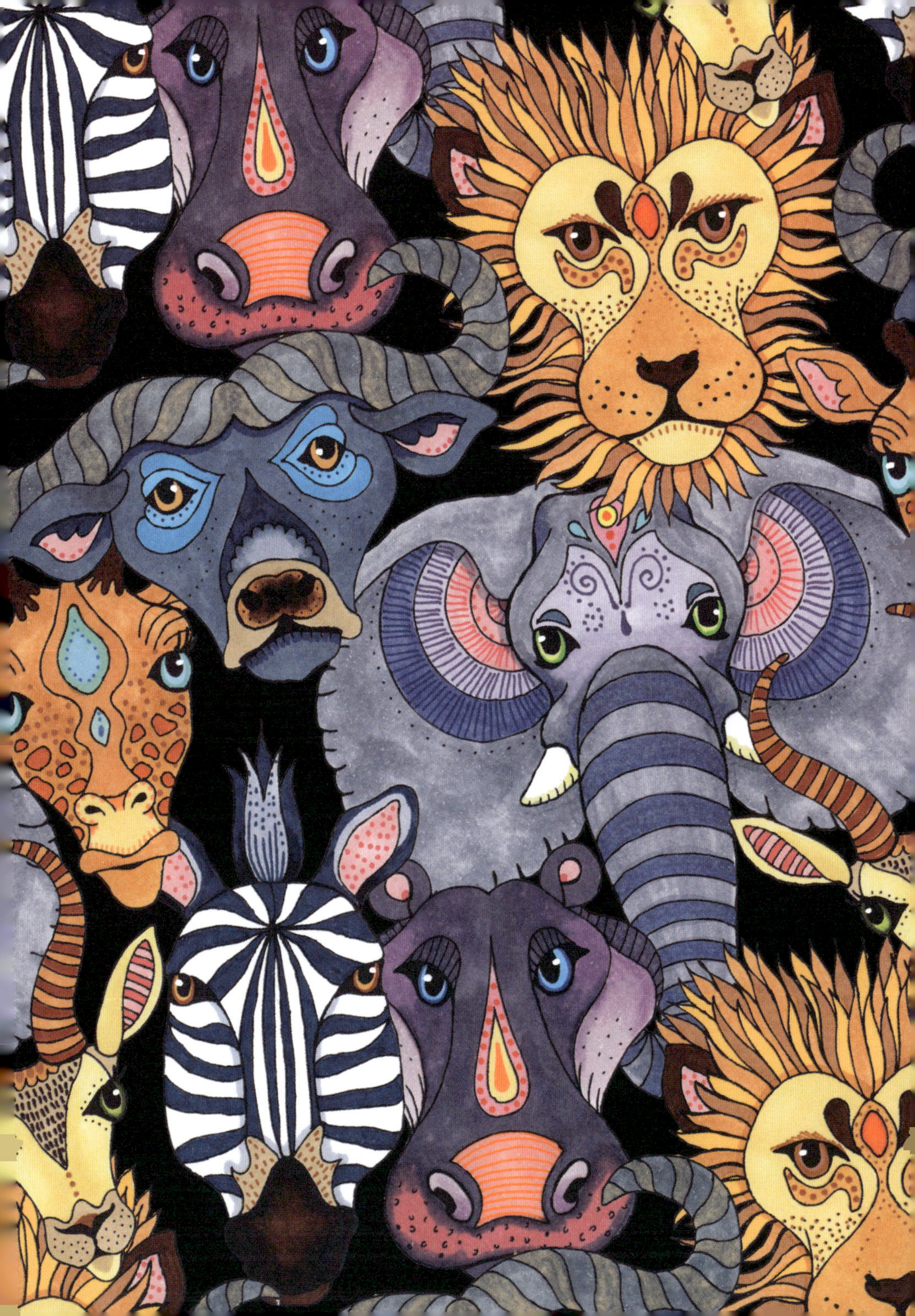

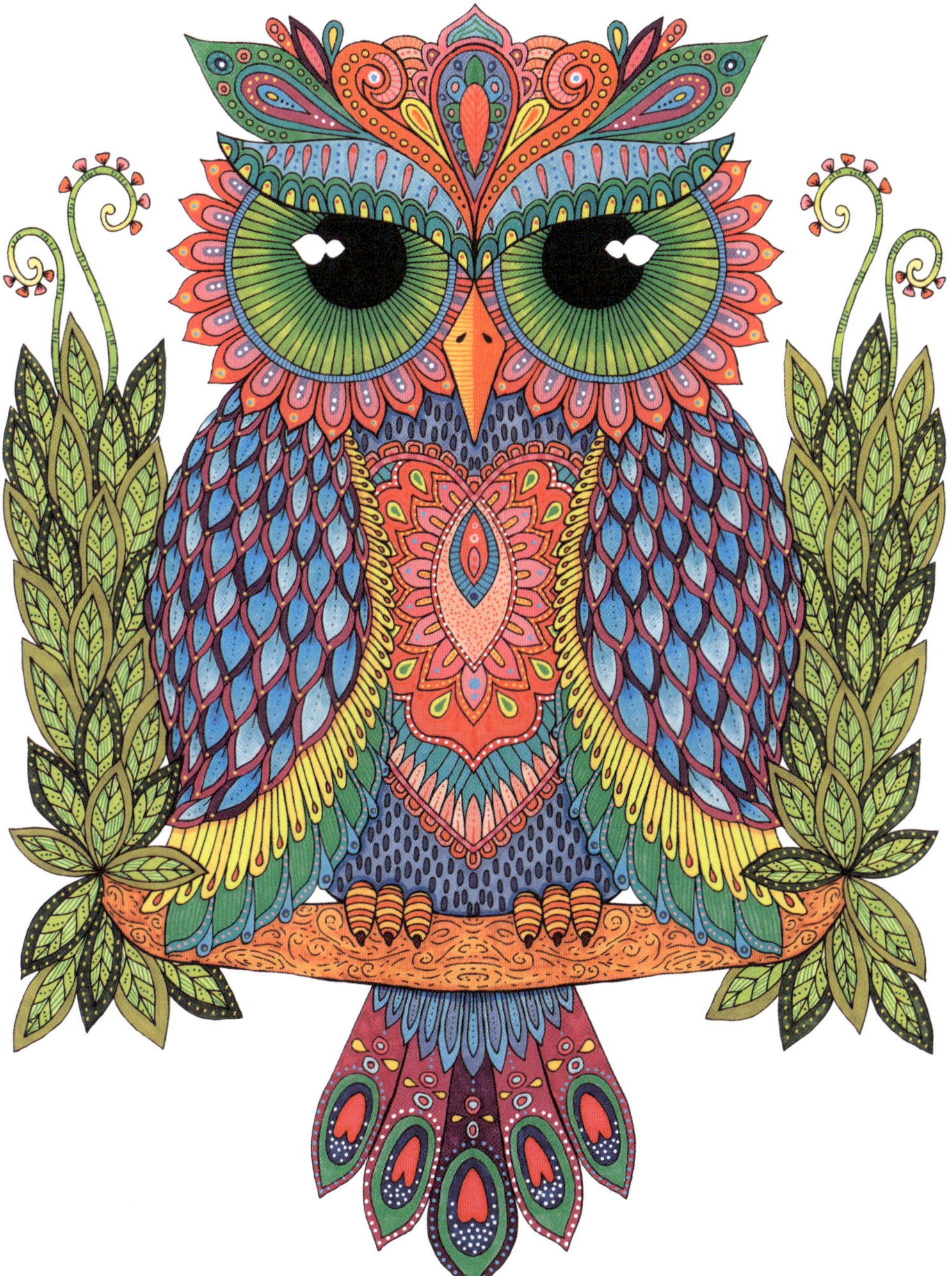

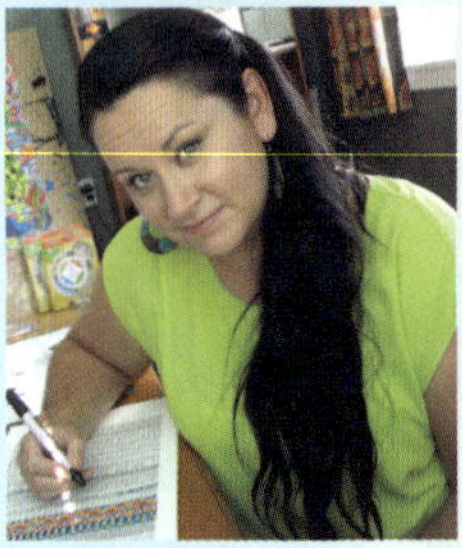

About the Artist

Angelea Van Dam of Hello Angel has drawn her entire life. This New Zealand artist is a graphic designer by trade, working out of her home as a freelancer. Her color style is every color under the sun and then she likes to pile on some more! Angelea wants to be in her studio making art almost all the time. It's what makes her happy. The fact that her art inspires others makes her doubly happy and motivates her to create so much more.

Color Your World with Hello Angel Coloring

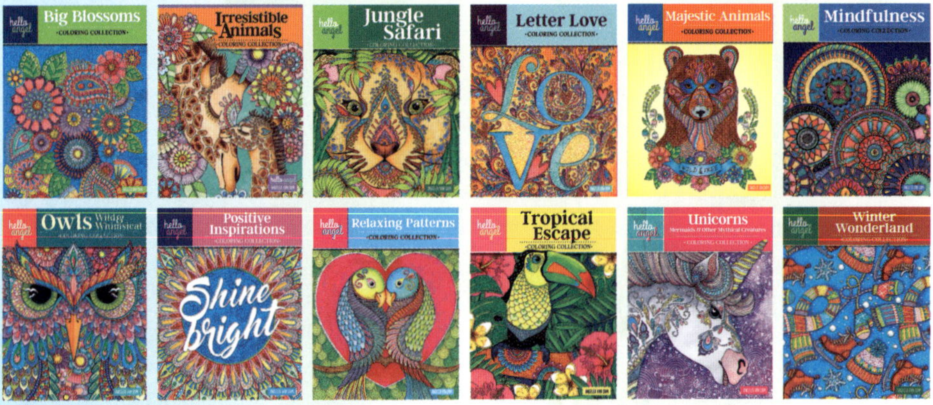
Big Blossoms
Irresistible Animals
Jungle Safari
Letter Love
Majestic Animals
Mindfulness
Owls
Positive Inspirations
Shine bright
Relaxing Patterns
Tropical Escape
Unicorns
Winter Wonderland

ISBN 978-1-64178-006-3

Fox Chapel Publishing makes every effort to use environmentally friendly paper for printing.

We are always looking for talented authors. To submit an idea, please send a brief inquiry to acquisitions@foxchapelpublishing.com.

Printed in China
First printing

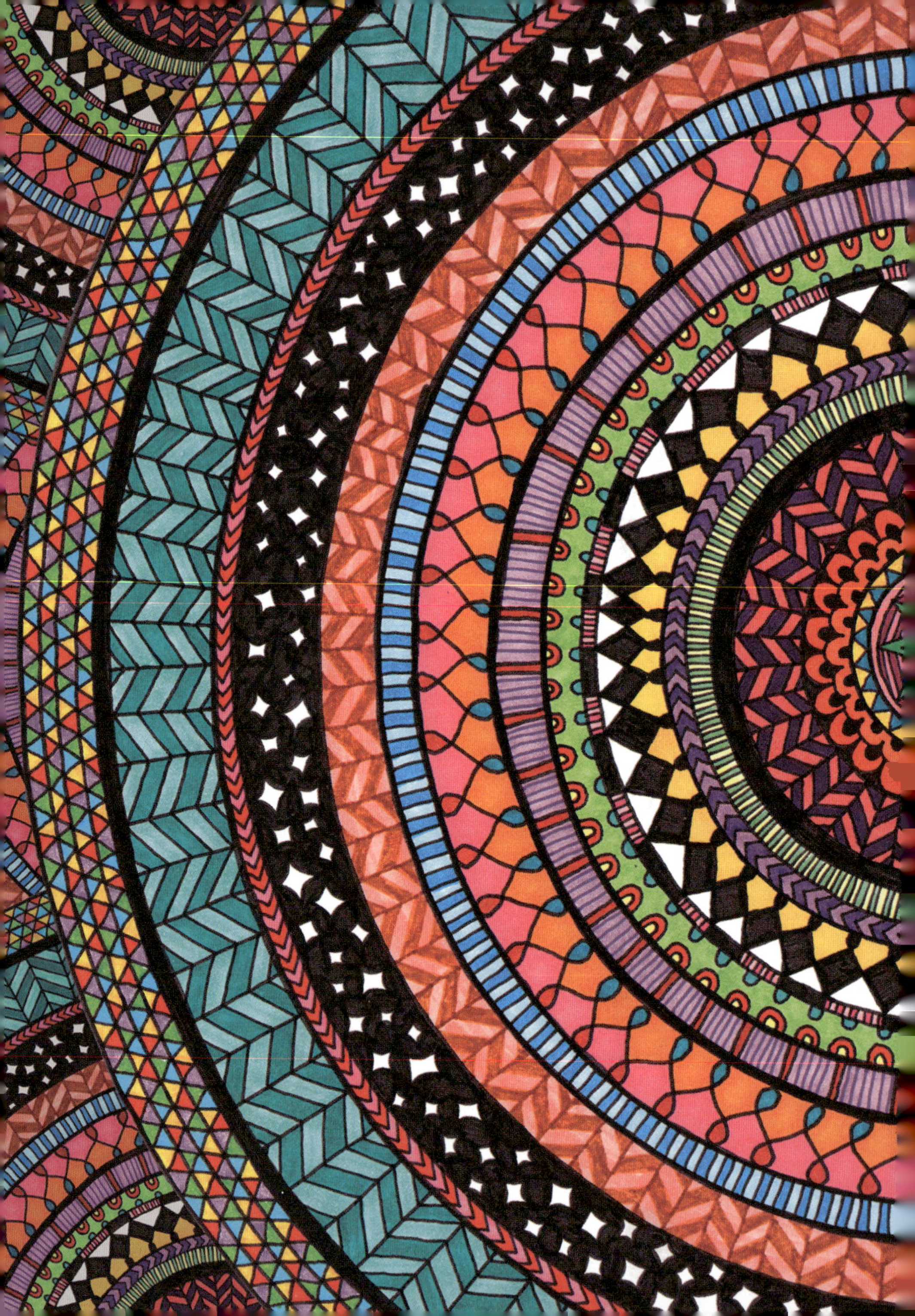